Beyond the 'Separate Self'

The End of Anxiety and Mental Suffering

A Simple Guide to Awakening

Based on the Meditations, Contemplations, and Experiences of Forty Years of Spiritual Search and Practice

by Colin Drake

Copyright © 2011 by Colin Drake

First Edition

All rights reserved. No part of this book shall be reproduced or transmitted, for commercial purposes, without written permission from the author.

Published by Colin Drake and Printed by www.lulu.com

Cover design and photography by the author.

ISBN: 978-0-9871655-0-3

Also by the same author:

A Light Unto Your Self
Self Discovery
Through
Investigation of Experience

Humanity Our Place in the Universe
The Central Beliefs
Of
The Worlds Religions

Poetry
From
Beyond The Separate Self

All of these titles are available as: e-books at www.nonduality.com and in hard copy at www.lulu.com or
http://www.lulu.com/spotlight/colin108atbigponddotcom

Dedications and Acknowledgements.

I would like to dedicate this book to the following people who have inspired, helped, supported, advised and encouraged me in my spiritual journey:

> My father John for his unmitigated cheerfulness, sense of humour and love of humanity.
> My mother Peggy for her love, care, and appreciation of the natural world.
> My sisters, Joy and Wendy, for their friendship, love, and dedication to the spiritual life.
> My partner Janet, who has been my spiritual companion for over thirty years, for her love, tolerance, companionship and loyalty.
> My spiritual friends, 'artist Ray', 'Krishnamurti John', 'madman Neil', George, Gary, Yarn, Claire and Michael, and many others, for the illuminating discussions we have had together.
> My e-book publisher, Jerry Katz, who believed in me enough to publish this book.
>
> Matthew O'Malveny who first taught yoga to me and reawakened my spiritual curiosity.
> Swami Satyananda Saraswati who initiated me and introduced me to the joys of the many different yogic paths and practices.
> Swamis Karmamurti and Bhaktimurti Saraswati for their living example of the yogic life and its many benefits.
> Sri Ramakrishna Paramahansa for his catholicity, teachings, ecstasy and amazing life.
> Pravajika Ajayaprana Mataji, who also initiated, inspired and encouraged me on my spiritual journey.
> Gangaji, who was the instrument of my first 'awakening', for the directness and simplicity of her teachings.
> Isaac Shapiro, who also shares the same directness of teaching, for his friendship and encouragement.
> Osho and Krishnamurti for their unique and 'enlightened' teachings.

Contents

Introduction..5
1. The Problem..9
2. Investigation of Experience............................17
3. Simply Free to Be..26
4. The Perceiver Not the Perceived....................40
5. Nothing to Achieve, Find or Get....................46
6. On 'This' and 'That'..52
7. Nothing Special..58
8. Home Is Where the Heart Is............................62
9. Nothing Matters..66
10. Relax into Self-Realization..............................71
11. Mantra as a Vehicle of Revelation..............75
12. Every Thought and Sensation Reveals Reality........80
13. Nothing to Do, No Problem to Solve.................84
14. So What? ... What Now?..................................88
15. All or Nothing...97
16. The Full Potential..102
17. The Best of All Worlds, Humanity at its Peak........112
18. Purpose and Meaning..117
19. The Absolute Reality..124
20. The Essential Self..150
21. Self-Liberation Through Naked Awareness..........172
Appendix - Spiritual Experience..........................180
Glossary..191
Index...196
Biography..207

Introduction

This book is designed to help its readers go 'beyond the separate self'; that is to free oneself from obsessive thinking and worrying about one's self-image, health, wealth, status, achievements, lack of achievements, past, future and ultimate survival. These are all caused by identifying oneself as an individual object in a universe of multiple objects, and also by comparing oneself with like objects (other people). How we identify ourselves is at the heart of how we view the world and our place in it. If we fail to correctly identify 'what we are' (in essence) then this leads to an unfulfilled life, with its consequent frustrations and mental suffering.

The discussions that follow are concerned with coming to a valid conclusion regarding self-identity, and then learning to operate from this level of being. This is to be achieved purely by investigating our existence, which comprises an unending stream of moment-to-moment experiences from birth to death. Even during sleep there is experience of dreams and sensations. If a sensation becomes strong enough it will wake one up. This investigation requires no dogma or belief systems, and these need to be put aside for the investigation to succeed.

The author, who had spent over thirty years in various Christian, Hindu and Yogic practices, only progressed (had the first real 'awakening') when he abandoned these and entered a deep investigation of the question 'Who am I?'. The appendix contains an account of this questioning, the experiences that it produced, and the insights that it revealed. The appendix also shows how the experiences, which resulted from the direct recognition of true self-identity, related back to the preceding belief system of the author. However, although these beliefs colour the experiences that follow the direct recognition, they are of no use in the investigation itself.

This is not to say that the religions of the world do not point to this same realization and chapter 19 attempts to show how they all do this in their own way. The problem is that the truth of this realization is so incredibly simple, one could say obvious, that the various religious traditions have been unable to accept such simplicity; so their followers, and commentators, have overlaid this simplicity with many levels of dogma, beliefs and philosophical systems.

Chapter 1 is devoted to a general discussion of the various problems associated with misidentifying oneself as an object, such as: self-obsession, self-loathing, selfishness, self-aggrandizement, self-importance, etc. The list is almost endless. This chapter also sets the framework for the investigations of those that follow, many of which read as if they are meditations or contemplations, which is exactly what they are. These stem directly from the author's direct investigations over a twelve year period since his first 'awakening'. They are given as pointers and aids for the reader's own investigations into, and contemplations on, the problem of self-identity. There is necessarily some duplication between them as what is being discussed is so simple. They are different 'takes' on the same simplicity, presenting the material in various ways whilst building upon what has been discovered, so some repetition is unavoidable. It should also be noted that each of these are, as far as is possible, stand-alone meditations or contemplations, thus needing to make sense by themselves. Therefore some sections of each will contain similar passages, so that they are relatively complete when read in isolation.

Chapter 2 gives the basic format for investigating one's direct moment-to-moment experience and is the basis for the chapters that follow. Chapter 3 was written on a seven day solitary retreat of investigation, meditation and contemplation in 2000. It represents the author's first attempt to discuss, in writing, the problem of self-identity, and has been published as a stand-alone pamphlet. Chapters 4 to 13 are further meditations and contemplations, each delving deeper into the nature of self-identity and 'reality'. Chapter 14 details how to live from the level of self-identity that has been discovered and the benefits of this. Chapter 15 highlights the importance of committing to this level to access the full potential of 'awakening'. Chapter 16 discusses this 'full potential' and shows how this truly is 'the end of anxiety and mental suffering'. Chapter 17 shows how humanity could live together in perfect peace and harmony by the realization of this deeper level of self-identity and the nature of reality, which have been revealed by one's investigations. Chapter 18 considers how living from this deeper level of self-identity makes life so enjoyable that no extra purpose or meaning is necessary. Chapter 19 studies how the religions of the world describe the Absolute Reality and compares this with what is discovered through direct investigation into the nature of moment-to-moment experience. It also shows how mystics of each religion have arrived at the same conclusion.

Chapter 20 shows how two seemingly opposing concepts of self-identity - 'essential self' and 'no essential self' - can ultimately lead to the same conclusion that is discovered by direct investigation of experience. It is a fairly detailed discussion of the Hindu and Buddhist concepts of self-identity, and it compares the various ideas that these religions contain. In simple language it offers an introductory insight into these two major world religions and may be useful for 'non-dualists' who regard the word 'Self' as the 'essential self' and are somewhat unhappy about the phrase 'separate self'. Chapter 21 shows how the discoveries made by direct investigation of experience tally with those given in the fourth chapter of *The Tibetan Book of the Dead*, 'Self-Liberation Through Seeing with Naked Awareness'.

If you have any questions, as you read the book, you can e-mail me at colin108@dodo.com.au . I am quite happy to clarify any points that you do not understand; however, I would rather not field questions on topics that are clearly covered in the text. If you are not sure it would be advisable to wait until you have finished the book, as you may well find that your question is answered.

Chapter One

The Problem

A general discussion on the problem of identifying oneself as an individual object in a universe of multiple objects. It also sets the framework for the investigations that follow which reveal a deeper level of being than that of thoughts and sensations.

The Problem

For most of us much of our waking time is spent in obsessive thinking about 'ourselves' and our relationships with other people. This is especially true when we are not working, using our minds in a productive activity; or when we are not relaxing in such a way that engages the mind such as reading a book, playing a game or watching a screen. For the mind is akin to an onboard-computer which is a wonderful tool for problem-solving, information storing, retrieval and processing, and evaluating the data provided by our senses. However, when it is not fully utilized it tends to search for other problems to solve, and if these are not presently available it tends to speculate about the future, delve into the past, or imagine in the present, creating non-existent problems which it then tries to solve!

Most people tend to identify with their mind, rather than seeing it as a tool, which creates myriad problems. This causes everything to be seen through the filter of the mind: its opinions, judgements, and self-interest. When this happens we cease to see things as they really are which lessens our ability to relate to the world in a natural healthy way. Imagine the problems it would cause if your computer decided that it was 'you' and coloured all the information it retrieved from the internet with its own arbitrary opinions and judgements. In this case you would be unable to rely on any of this information, and if you did then any decisions made using this would be liable to be faulty.

In the above example 'you' are obviously not the computer but the perceiver of the data provided by the computer and all of its multimedia functionality. In the same way, we have a deeper level of being than the mind (thoughts and mental images) and body (physical sensations), which is also the perceiver of this 'data'. However, when we identify at the surface level of mind/body we are unaware of this and tend to suffer due to the shortcomings of our mind/body. This is akin to suffering because our computer is not the most up-to-date, fastest attractive model available.

This is exactly what most of us do, worrying about our body-image and mental capacity and ability. We tend to expand our concept of self-identity to include an imaginary self-image consisting of our physical appearance, mental ability, status, occupation, position in society, family situation, achievements, lack of achievements, ambitions, hopes, fears, memories and projections into the future. Not only do we consider this to be who or what we are, and continually obsess about this, but we also spend large periods of time comparing this with the equally erroneous images we have formed of other people we relate to.

So we have identified ourselves as an imaginary object, in a universe of separate objects, which we then compare with other imaginary objects! This is bound to lead to confusion, suffering and an increased feeling of separation, which is exacerbated by the fact that we do not even see these other objects as they actually are, but as we imagine them to be through the filter of our mind's opinions, judgements and self-interest.

The Problem

To free ourselves from this nightmarish scenario and the continual obsession with the 'separate self' we imagine ourselves to be, we need to connect with the deeper level of our being as the 'subject' rather than an 'object', where we are the perceiver of our thoughts and sensations. This level is ever-present as there is continual awareness of our thoughts and sensations. Whilst we identify with the mind this level is overlooked; the mind continues the vicious circle of obsessive thinking by processing these thoughts and sensations and relating them to the imaginary self-image that it has concocted.

However, we can easily escape from this vicious circle by simply investigating the nature and relationship of these thoughts and sensations and our awareness of them. When this is fully accomplished we discover that, at the deepest level, we are the perceiver of these thoughts and sensations. These are just ephemeral objects which come and go, leaving the perceiver totally unaffected, in the same way that the sky is unaffected by the clouds which scud across it, or the ocean is undisturbed by the waves and swells that appear on its surface.

This is what this book is designed to achieve, to take one beyond the 'separate self' we have imagined ourselves to be. In this we discover that most of our worries have no foundation for they are just the mind projecting into the future, wallowing in the past, or obsessing over the imaginary self-image it has conjured up. Once the mind is put in its place - as the servant and not the master - we start to see things as they truly are, and to recognize not only the deeper level of being within ourselves but also to recognize this in those around us. Then we see that our self-image and the images we have created of other people are all just illusions. At this deeper level we relate to others in a much more loving, wholesome way, for it becomes clear that there is in fact no separation between ourselves and others, as at this level we share the same constant conscious subjective presence.

This is not a question of belief or imagination but of discovery by direct investigation, and for this to be effective we need to put aside all belief systems and acquired knowledge concerning who we are at the underlying level beyond thoughts and sensations. The only knowledge of this that is valid is that which is revealed to each one of us by direct experience. The easiest way for this direct experience to occur is by enquiring into the nature of experience itself, and for this enquiry to be effective we need to start from the position of believing and knowing nothing.

The chapters that follow are aids to this enquiry, and as such should not just be read and intellectually considered but need to be taken slowly, step by step, not moving onto the next step until one fully 'sees' the step that is being considered. This does not mean to say that one needs to agree with each statement, as any investigation is personal, but one needs to understand what is being said. They map the author's own investigations, over a twelve-year period, and are given in the order in which they occurred. They each stem directly from a prolonged period of meditation and contemplation, and chart a growing understanding, through experiencing and seeing, of the nature of reality and our place within it. As such they need to be taken in the order given, as each one builds on what has been 'seen' in the preceding chapters. Also to get the most out of each chapter one needs to spend some time contemplating it until one 'feels' what it is pointing to; if a chapter is just read without due attention then its significance may well be missed. If, however, the reader becomes somewhat impatient because they truly feel that they have 'got' what is being offered, then they can go on to chapter 14 'So What ... What Now?', and return to the earlier unread chapters, when and as they wish. It would be unadvisable to do this until one has finished chapter 4 'The Perceiver Not the Perceived'.

Before starting we need to discuss the nature of awareness itself. It is obvious that we would not 'know' (be aware of) our own perceptions without awareness being present. This does not mean that we are always conscious of each one of them, as this is dictated by where we put our attention, or upon what we focus our mind. However, all sensations detected by the body are there in awareness, and we can readily become conscious of them by turning our attention to them. It is also true that our thoughts and mental images immediately appear in awareness, but these require less attention to be seen as they occur in the mind itself. So awareness is like the screen on which all of our thoughts and sensations appear, and the mind becomes conscious of these by focusing on them. Take, for example, what happens when you open your eyes and look at a beautiful view: everything seen immediately appears in awareness, but for the mind to make anything of this it needs to focus upon certain elements of what is seen. 'There is an amazing tree', 'wow look at that eagle', 'what a stunning sky', etc. To be sure, you may just make a statement like 'what a beautiful view', but this does not in itself say much and is so self-evident as to be not worth saying!

The point is that the mind is a tool for problem-solving, information storing, retrieval and processing, and evaluating the data provided by our senses. It achieves this by focusing on specific sensations, thoughts or mental images that are present in awareness, and 'processing' these. In fact we only truly see 'things as they are' when they are not seen through the filter of the mind, and this occurs when what is encountered is able to 'stop the mind'. For instance we have all had glimpses of this at various times in our lives, often when seeing a beautiful sunset, a waterfall or some other wonderful natural phenomenon. These may seem other-worldly or intensely vivid, until the mind kicks in with any evaluation when everything seems to return to 'normal'. In fact nature is much more vivid and alive when directly perceived, and the more we identify with the 'perceiver', as awareness itself, the more frequently we see things 'as they are'.

However, as long as we identify with our imaginary self-image we are always trying to better ourselves, achieve more - knowledge, possessions, power, fame, etc. - polish this self-image and generally build ourselves up. This tends to make us live in the future and stops us living fully in the present moment. The other side of this coin is to live

The Problem

in regret as to what might have been, self-loathing, melancholy or nostalgia and yearning for the past. This, once again, stops us seeing 'what is' here and now, either by making us live in the past or by the mind spinning on our failures and lack of self-worth.

The following chapters are aids in the investigation of one's moment-to-moment experience. These are designed to enable you to discover this deeper level of being where you are truly the 'perceiver' not the 'perceived'.

Chapter Two

Investigation of Experience

A straightforward and direct method to investigate one's moment-to-moment experience. The discoveries that are made form the basis of the chapters that follow. However, don't worry if you don't fully 'get' what is being pointed to, for the following chapters point to the same outcome in different ways.

Investigation of Experience

Below follows a simple method to investigate the nature of reality starting with one's day-to-day experience. Each step should be considered until one experiences, or 'sees', its validity before moving on to the following step. If you reach a step where you do not find this possible, continue on regardless in the same way, and hopefully the flow of the investigation will make this step clear. By all means examine each step critically but with an open mind, for if you only look for 'holes' that's all you will find!

1. Consider the following statement: 'Life, for each of us, is just a series of moment-to-moment experiences'. These experiences start when we are born and continue until we die, rushing headlong after each other, so that they seem to merge into a whole that we call 'my life'. However, if we stop to look we can readily see that, for each of us, every moment is just an experience.

2. Any moment of experience has only three elements: thoughts (including all mental images), sensations (everything sensed by the body and its sense organs) and awareness of these thoughts and sensations. Emotions and feelings are a combination of thought and sensation.

3. Thoughts and sensations are ephemeral, that is they come and go, and are objects, i.e. 'things' that are perceived.

4. Awareness is the constant subject, the 'perceiver' of thoughts and sensations and that which is always present. Even during sleep there is awareness of dreams and of the quality of that sleep; and there is also awareness of sensations; if a sensation becomes strong enough, such as a sound or uncomfortable sensation, one will wake up.

5. All thoughts and sensations appear in awareness, exist in awareness, and subside back into awareness. Before any particular thought or sensation there is effortless awareness of 'what is': the sum of all thoughts and sensations occurring at any given instant. During the thought or sensation in question there is effortless awareness of it within 'what is'. Then when it has gone there is still effortless awareness of 'what is'.

6. So the body/mind is experienced as a flow of ephemeral objects appearing in this awareness, the ever present subject. For each of us any external object or thing is experienced as a combination of thought and sensation, i.e. you may see it, touch it, know what it is called, and so on. The point is that for us to be aware of anything, real or imaginary, requires thought about and/or sensation of that thing and it is awareness of these thoughts and sensations that constitutes our experience.

7. Therefore this awareness is the constant substratum in which all things appear to arise, exist and subside. In addition, all living things rely on awareness of their environment to exist and their behaviour is directly affected by this. At the level of living cells and above this is

self-evident, but it has been shown that even electrons change their behaviour when (aware of) being observed! Thus this awareness exists at a deeper level than body/mind (and matter/energy[1]) and *we are this awareness*!

8. This does not mean that at a surface level we are not the mind and body, for they arise in, are perceived by and subside back into awareness, which is the deepest and most fundamental level of our being. However, if we choose to identify with this deepest level – awareness - (the perceiver) rather than the surface level, mind/body (the perceived), then thoughts and sensations are seen for what they truly are, just ephemeral objects which come and go, leaving awareness itself totally unaffected.

9. Next investigate this awareness itself to see whether its properties can be determined.
Firstly what is apparent is that this awareness is effortlessly present and effortlessly aware. It requires no effort by the mind/body and thoughts and sensations cannot make it vanish however hard they try.

10. Next, this awareness is choicelessly present and choicelessly aware. Once again it requires no choice of the mind/body and they cannot block it however they try. For example, if you have a toothache there is effortless awareness of it and the mind/body cannot choose for this not to be the case. You may think that this is bad news but it is not so: can

---

[1] The theory of relativity, and string theory, show that matter and energy are synonymous.

you imagine if you had to make a choice whether you would like to be aware of every sensation that the body experiences? In fact be grateful that there is no effort or choice involved for awareness just to be - such ease and simplicity - which is not surprising for you are this awareness!

11. It can be seen then, that for each of us this awareness is omnipresent; we never experiences a time or place when it is not present. Once again be grateful that the mind/body is never required to search for this awareness; it is just always there, which of course is not surprising for at the deepest level we are this awareness.

12. Next, notice that this awareness is absolutely still for it is aware of the slightest movement of body or mind. For example, we all know that to be completely aware of what is going on around us in a busy environment we have to be completely still, just witnessing the activity.

13. In the same vein this awareness is totally silent as it is aware of the slightest sound and the smallest thought.

14. In fact this awareness is totally without attributes for all attributes occur in and are noticed by their lack, i.e. sounds occur in silence, exist in silence, are noticed by their contrast to silence, and disappear back into silence; forms occur in space, exist in space, are noticed by their contrast to space, disappear back into space, and so on.

15. It can be easily seen that this awareness is totally pure; it is unaffected by whatever occurs in it, in the same way that a cinema screen is unaffected by any movie shown on it, however gross or violent. In fact no 'thing' can taint awareness; for by definition awareness cannot be affected by any 'thing', as all 'things' are just ephemeral objects which appear in, exist in and finally disappear back into awareness, the constant subject.

16. This awareness is omniscient; everything appears to arise in it, to exist in it, is known by it and to subside back into it.

17. Finally, it seems that this awareness is forever radiant; it illuminates whatever occurs in it, thus the mind can see it, i.e. become conscious of it.

18. When one identifies with this awareness, there is nothing (in terms of enlightenment or awakening) to achieve, or struggle towards, for how can one achieve what one already is?
All that is required is for the mind to recognize that one is this awareness.

19. When one identifies with this awareness there is nothing to find, for how can one find what cannot be lost? All that is required is for the mind to stop overlooking what is always present, that which perceives the mind and body.

20. When one identifies with this awareness, there is nothing to desire, long for or get, for how can one get what already is? All that is required is for the mind to realize that which one already is: pure awareness.

So now we have reached the 'Pure, radiant, still, silent, omnipresent, omniscient, ocean of effortless, choiceless, attributeless awareness' which we all are! Give up all striving, seeking and desiring, and just identify with This which you already are. Identification with This, rather than with body/mind (thought/sensations), gives instant peace, for awareness is always still and silent, totally unaffected by whatever appears in it.

Although we, in essence, are 'The pure, radiant, still, silent, omnipresent, omniscient, ocean of effortless, choiceless, attributeless awareness' it is impossible to experience this: we can know it or realize it but it is beyond the realm of experience. This is because all experience appears in This, exists in This and dissolves back into This. In much the same way that you do not see the cinema screen whilst the movie is playing, this pure screen of awareness cannot be seen by the mind, i.e. experienced, whilst the movie of mind/body is playing on it. The only way it is possible to see the screen is when no movie is playing, but as *experience is the movie* this pure screen of awareness is always outside of the realm of experience. However, recognition of oneself as this 'pure, radiant, still, silent, omnipresent, omniscient, ocean of effortless, choiceless, attributeless, awareness' may evoke many experiences such as bliss, joy, relaxation (what a relief that there's no individual 'me me me'), a lifting of a great burden, i.e. enlightenment in the literal sense of the word, universal love etc. These experiences vary greatly from person to person and are ultimately irrelevant as the recognition and realization of one's own essential nature is the crucial factor for attaining freedom.

Note that although we cannot experience our essence, we can absolutely know it* just as we know, without a doubt, that the screen is there (when we watch a movie). Then however terrifying, gripping or moving the movie is we are not shaken because we know it is a movie. We still enjoy it, in fact we enjoy it even more, because it is just pure entertainment and we are not totally identified with it. In the same way, once we know our essential nature, life can be seen as a movie and enjoyed as such without identifying ourselves as being trapped in it. Thus, although we cannot experience our essence, once we recognize it all of our experiences are transformed by no longer identifying with them but just enjoying them, or accepting them as ephemeral states which come and go. When viewed like this, thoughts and sensations lose their power to overwhelm us, as we stop buying into them as indicators of who or what we are. They are just like waves on the ocean or clouds in the sky, which appear and disappear leaving the ocean or the sky unaffected.

*Just as you could not see a movie without the screen, you could not experience anything without awareness, for without that what would there be to experience? For without that we would see nothing (there would be no awareness of what was seen), hear nothing, feel nothing, taste nothing, smell nothing and not know our own thoughts! In fact, experience on any level would not be possible.

Chapter Three

Simply Free to Be

Effortless Awareness is our Real State – Ramana Maharshi

That which you truly are, Pure Awareness – Sogyal Rinpoche

Here is a self-contained discussion of the problem of Self-Identity, which contains an earlier more basic method of investigating experience. It also shows how other prominent thinkers have pointed to Pure Awareness and acts as a precursor for the chapters that follow.

Can you imagine living free from fears, beliefs, ambitions, desires, conditionings, etc.? That is to say that although these will continue to come up one will no longer be compelled, or constrained, by them; so that one is just 'simply free to be' with no shoulds and shouldn'ts, cans and cannots, past and future, totally here now in this moment. This is the natural easy way of living that seems to be so rare in the modern world. We are so conditioned to becoming something, making our mark on the world, improving ourselves, that we are continually striving, intent on some wonderful future or wallowing in the past, and this stops us living totally in the present moment.

Why is it that we allow this to happen and thus lose the joy of spontaneous living? It seems to me that this is due to misidentification of ourselves with some imaginary self-image which we have fostered and have been conditioned to foster by our society. This self-image is made up of our physical appearance, mental prowess, belief systems, ambitions, past achievements and status in the world. It is this purely imaginary self-image that causes all our psychological suffering. For with no self-image, but just 'being' moment to moment, there is no fear of losing face, of not achieving or of failure as there is nothing to protect.

At this point you may say if we are not this self-image what are we? The natural answer is that we are the mind/body, but surely this belief is the beginning of identifying with a self-image and the cause of all of our problems. If we look we can see that the mind is just a thought stream that is continually changing. Without a thought there is literally 'no-mind'. Although thoughts hold us in their sway and appear to have tremendous power they are, in essence, ephemeral and without substance. Our body is also ephemeral in that it is continually changing and will surely die.

So if we identify ourselves as being mind/body we are identifying ourselves as being nothing but an ever-moving thought stream in a structure that will indeed perish. This could well lead to tremendous fear, uncertainty, nihilism and despair. This is where religion comes in to placate and comfort us in the belief in God and the 'soul' or 'spirit' which lives on after death. Belief in this can be very helpful but as it is just a belief it is subject to doubt and loss of faith, which leaves us back at square one.

What would be even more helpful would be to discover, experientially, that changeless permanent 'ground of being' which at our source we truly are. Direct experience is the key here as that can be trusted whereas beliefs come and go. What's more, if this direct experience were readily available to each one of us then the problem would be solved.

The easiest method is by 'self-enquiry' which means to sit enquiring deeply into the question "Who am I?". The aim of this enquiring is to look deeper than the mind/body and see if you can discover this changeless 'ground of being'.

To make this even easier I would like to point out the following:

If you sit quietly you can easily notice that:

There is effortless awareness of every thought.

There is effortless awareness of every sound.

There is effortless awareness of every sight.

There is effortless awareness of every taste.

There is effortless awareness of every smell.

There is effortless awareness of every feeling.

There is effortless awareness of every touch.

This awareness encompasses every mind/body experience, for they appear in it.

Deeper than thoughts (mind) and sensory experiences (body) *you are this awareness.*

This awareness is effortless and choiceless as it requires no effort and it is choicelessly present.

This awareness is omnipresent. If you investigate you will find that it is (and has been) always present wherever you are. Even during sleep there is awareness of dreams, and of the quality of that sleep.

This awareness is absolutely still as it is aware of the slightest movement of body/mind.

This awareness is utterly silent as it is aware of the smallest sound, the slightest thought.

Every mind/body experience appears in this awareness, exists in this awareness and disappears back into this awareness.

At the deepest level you are this pure, still, silent, boundless, changeless awareness.

The great English philosopher C. E .M. Joad, on his deathbed, did not understand this and so he sent for P. D. Ouspensky (Gurdjeiff's great disciple), who explained: 'It is a very simple matter. You just close your eyes and remember one thing: whatever is going on before your inner eye is the mind, and the presence in front of which the mind is passing is no-mind [pure awareness]'. [2]

So this inner eye, that which sees all that is going on in the mind and the body, is the deeper level of pure awareness. This is a constant witnessing presence which is unaffected by what is witnessed. The mind collects its data from the totality of what is witnessed, that is from the thoughts and sensations that appear on the 'screen' of pure awareness.

The famous French philosopher Rene Descartes, from whom came the phrase 'I think therefore I am', points to this when he says: 'We clearly perceive the mind, apart from the body and vice-versa we can perceive the body apart from the mind'.[3] From this he concludes that the mind and body are separate intimately connected entities and identifies himself with the mind. However, what he overlooks here is the fact that he has identified himself with the object, in fact one of the two objects

---

[2] S. Rajneesh, *Ta Hui*, 1987, Cologne, p. 52
[3] J. Cottingham, *Meditations on a First Philosophy*, 1996, Cambridge, p. 10

(mind and body) and not the subject (the perceiver). Later in defending his position he points directly to awareness when he says: 'We know it by that internal awareness which always precedes reflective knowledge. This awareness of one's thoughts and existence is innate in all men.'[4] However, he did not then come to the logical conclusion that *one is this awareness* but continued to identify with the mind, which unfortunately is the usual condition.

Therefore awareness, which is what you truly are, is that which perceives the mind, i.e. every thought. The mind (thoughts) is just an object in awareness, ephemeral, subject to constant change and finally death, as is the body. Pure awareness is changeless and eternal and is what we all, at the deepest level, are. Any self-image you may have is an illusion as it is also just an object in awareness and is ephemeral, constantly changing, which will also be destroyed on the death of the mind/body. In fact, of course, the whole physical world is an illusion as that too is constantly changing and will also finally cease to be!

Naturally on the physical level we still have to live in this world and will be confronted with many problems. But most of our problems are psychological and of our own making. Once we realize that we are not any self-image and definitely not the mind then things fall into perspective. The past stops haunting us, as from the point of view of pure awareness it doesn't exist. Any thoughts or emotions we may have about it are just ephemeral objects which come and go. Our true

---

[4] Ibid. p. 69

identity, pure awareness, is totally silent and still, unaffected by thoughts and emotions.

This is also completely true of any worries we may have about the future. These are also only thoughts, many of which may turn out to be invalid, appearing in awareness. The most powerful way to overcome psychological suffering is when it occurs to ask the question 'Who is suffering?' and see if you can find a 'who' that is suffering. There is awareness of suffering, certainly, but is this awareness, which is who you are, suffering? The only sufferer is the mind, which created the suffering and which is just a stream of thoughts.

I will give you a personal example of this which occurred recently. My wife and I had not been getting on due to her criticizing me and my reacting to this. So finally I said to her 'You don't think much of me do you?' After some thought she replied 'probably not …' Whereupon my mind ran with 'after 30 years of marriage and my wife doesn't think much of me. This is not much to build a relationship on. Maybe I should get out now…' I was then struck with the realization that as a body/mind I didn't think much of myself either! But from the point of view of pure awareness, which is what we both are, what we think is irrelevant. If we take the stream of thoughts to be real, instead of just an object in awareness, then all sorts of complications and suffering ensue. In my case I could have split a perfectly happy home, leaving my two sons and wife whom I love. As soon as I had this realization I stopped reacting and she stopped criticizing me!

So much of our lives are governed by our self-image and the image society has of us and it's all rubbish! From the point of view of reality, pure awareness, none of it matters. The only thing that matters is living fully in the present moment. This happens by seeing everything as it truly is, in pure awareness, and not through the narrow filter of our mind and its conditioning. This is to be done by putting the mind in its proper place as an instrument of awareness, as are all of our senses, and not as who we are. Then things can be seen with no-mind (or a still mind) and be perceived in their true glory. The mind can be invited to comment on them and analyse them if this is so desired. But it is only being used as an instrument. The mind is actually a wonderful power and is of immense use in negotiating the physical world. The problems only occur when we identify with it as who we are. It is indeed a beautiful servant but a terrible master…

So when we truly ask the question 'Who am I?' we find no thing. We may realize that we are pure awareness but this is not a thing. It is that in which all things appear, exist and finally disappear. This realization of being nothing has wonderful consequences. For our self-image building is a running from the possibility of being nothing. On finally realizing that we are in fact nothing all images of ourselves and others crumble into dust. This does not cause suffering however, but only joy and bliss as we realize ourselves to be much greater than any thing. In fact we are that ground of being in which all things appear, exist and disappear.

The consequences of this are truly amazing and totally freeing, for when you have no self-image you are psychologically invulnerable. As pure awareness we are obviously invulnerable for although this body/mind will die awareness continues. But to be psychologically invulnerable means that mental suffering totally ceases. This does not mean that pain ceases but the suffering caused by stewing on the pain does. I will give you another personal example from the recent past.

In the last few years I have become an adept at failure. My twenty year-old business has been slowly dying. I set up a new business which has been a total failure. I arranged for a tour by a realized master only for that to be cancelled. I then arranged for a meeting by video-conferencing only for that to be cancelled. I finally decided to hold my own meeting to proclaim this truth that I am writing. I informed over 700 people by mail or e-mail, advertised in three newspapers and had the meeting announced at the local Theosophical Society, which was to be the venue. After all that only one person showed up! As I knew her we just went to her house for a cup of tea, and my reaction was to find it really funny. There was no disappointment or upset, just humour and almost a sense of relief. In fact I would have to say that I find failure as interesting as success and I can only put this down to a lack of self-image. When one realizes that one is truly no-thing but only pure awareness, what is there to be affected by any events in life? This leads to total non-attachment, but as a by-product not a discipline. In fact nearly all of the disciplines which are meant to lead to enlightenment are actually by-products of it. I would say that the first thing to do is to wake up to who you really are and all of these come naturally. For example:

Non-attachment: I have already dealt with this. Pure awareness being totally unaffected by anything occurring within it.

Compassion: When you fully realize that all body/minds are just instruments of pure awareness then all appear as oneself. For there is, in essence, no difference. This realization naturally leads to compassion and love for all beings.

This may all sound incredibly simple, almost too good to be true, and it is. In fact the absolute simplicity of it is what has kept it a secret. The mind is so used to complication that such simplicity is immediately rejected in its constant search for peace, security and fulfilment. This is an absolute joke for if it would only stop and see it would find that these are already present!

This truth has actually been discovered by many of the great masters of the past: Lao-Tzu, Buddha, Krishna, Christ, etc… It is indicated in many of the holy scriptures. The problem is that their followers, being unable to accept such total simplicity, have overlaid it with mental complication and built up dogma and belief systems around it. As all of the scriptures have been written by the followers and not the masters, they reflect this complication and dogma. Thus the truth tends to be hidden, but it may be found by alert investigation.

So if you have discovered this truth, what now? As instruments of pure awareness, which is what our body/minds are, the only purpose is to live fully in each and every moment. The by-products of this, non-attachment and compassion, will ensure that we live in a useful, peaceful, helpful way. In fact once you have discovered that you are just pure awareness and you see the mental suffering around you, the natural tendency is to wish to alleviate all of this mess of unnecessary suffering by pointing as many people as possible to this so simple truth.

There are many of us engaged in this and vast numbers of people have glimpsed this truth. The problem is that due to the relentless pressure of the mind and identification with the mind (ego) many of these have turned from it. Make no mistake; the mind in control (ego) will not relinquish its power without a tremendous struggle. It will immediately dismiss this truth as being too simple, or say if it is so simple why aren't we all self-realized? The simple reason, of course, is due to misidentification of ourselves as the mind! If it does finally accept it the mind will then try to co-opt this truth for its own use, always trying to reassert its control. The simple solution to this is, when it comes to reality, *don't believe a single thought.* Just rely on immediate direct experience, and this direct experience that you are awareness can be had instantly. As soon as the mind carries on with its doubts, questions and tricks, notice that you are effortlessly aware of every thought. If you then just watch the thoughts from pure awareness, without following a single one, they soon quieten down and give up. This is an ongoing process but it is no cause for despondency. For every time this occurs these negative thoughts can make you turn to awareness itself and in awareness there is only serenity and peace ... In fact, in the same way, every single thing in existence is a pointer towards awareness. For everything perceived appears in this pure awareness that you are.

Although there is no need for this, I enjoy sitting quietly every morning, before the activity of the day and noticing that:

> There is effortless awareness of every thought.
> There is effortless awareness of every sound.
> There is effortless awareness of every sight.
> There is effortless awareness of every taste.
> There is effortless awareness of every smell.
> There is effortless awareness of every feeling.
> There is effortless awareness of every touch.

In fact this awareness encompasses every mind/body experience and *I am this* awareness!

> This awareness is effortless and choiceless as it requires no effort and is choicelessly present.
> This awareness is omnipresent.
> This awareness is absolutely still as it is aware of the slightest movement of body/mind.
> This awareness is utterly silent as it is aware of the smallest sound, the slightest thought.

Every mind/body experience appears in this awareness, exists in the awareness and disappears back into this awareness.

As this awareness there is nothing to achieve, for how can I achieve what I already am?
As this awareness there is nothing to find, for how can I find what I cannot lose?
As this awareness there is nothing to desire, or get, for how can I get what I already have?

This is not used as a mantra or an affirmation but as a living experience and it makes it easier for me to be vigilant in the day. The touchstone, for me, is that as soon as there is any mental suffering I am misidentifying myself as mind/body/mental-image. Then I can either ask 'who is suffering?' or I can instantly see that I am that which is aware of suffering.

So you may well now ask what of the various spiritual paths with such wonderful things as angels, avatars, channelled masters, spirit guides, visions, etc. These all may well exist and be experienced but, once again, they are only objects appearing in awareness! If you take note of what they are saying, sifting the sugar from the sand, you will find that they too are pointing to this pure awareness. Let me reiterate that anything you experience through the body/mind is just an object appearing in pure awareness; and, as previously pointed out, these experiences point to this awareness. And you are this pure, omnipresent, still, silent eternal awareness! As this you are *simply free to be*.

Chapter Four

The Perceiver Not the Perceived

This chapter points directly to the fact that one is the subject - that which perceives - rather than the object - that which is perceived - in every moment of experience.

The Perceiver Not the Perceived

Sri Nisargadatta promotes a process of *neti neti*, in which one investigates one's being, discarding the non-essential as 'not this not this', so that eventually one will come to That which is non-discardable, the essence that one truly is. About this process he said:

> To know what you are, you must first investigate and know what you are not. Discover all that you are not - body, feelings, thoughts, time, space, this or that -nothing which you can perceive can be you. The very act of perceiving shows that you are not what you perceive.[5]

The point is that one is the perceiver - that which becomes aware of - and not the perceived - those objects of which one becomes aware.

This process may seem to be interminable as there are an almost infinite number of things that one is not. However, it can be accomplished very quickly by considering the nature of every experience that we have. Firstly if we look we can easily see that our life is composed of a series of moment-to-moment experiences, and in any given moment of direct experience there are only three elements: thoughts (including all mental images), sensations (everything detected by the senses) and awareness of these thoughts and sensations. All thoughts and sensations are ephemeral objects (the perceived) which appear in this awareness (the perceiver) which is the constant subject. So at a deeper level than the

---

[5] Nisargadatta Maharaj, *I Am That*, 1997, Durham NY, p. vi

ever-changing objects (thoughts and sensations) we are this constant subject, awareness itself.

To put this in a slightly different way, we can easily notice that every thought and sensation occurs in awareness, exists in awareness and dissolves back into awareness. Before any thought, or sensation, awareness is present; during the thought, or sensation, awareness is present and after it has gone awareness is still present. Also for each of us any external object (or thing) is experienced as a combination of thought and sensation, i.e. you see it, touch (feel) it, know what it is called, etc. Therefore in our direct experience everything arises in, exists in and subsides back into awareness itself.

So the mind, which is experienced as a flow of thoughts, and the body which is experienced as a flow of sensations, are both flows of ephemeral objects. This does not mean that at a surface level we are not the mind and body, for they arise in, are perceived by and subside back into awareness, which is the deepest and most fundamental level of our being. However, if we choose to identify with this deepest level, awareness (the perceiver) rather than the surface level, mind/body (the perceived), then thoughts and sensations are seen for what they truly are, just ephemeral objects which come and go, leaving awareness itself totally unaffected. For by definition awareness cannot be affected by any 'thing', as all 'things' are just ephemeral objects which appear in, exist in and finally disappear back into awareness, the constant subject.

Awareness can also be defined as universal consciousness when it is totally at rest, completely still; aware of everything that is occurring within it. We have already seen that awareness (consciousness) is still, and is in fact the 'stillness' relative to which any movement can be known. Every 'thing' that is occurring in consciousness is a manifestation of cosmic energy, for the string theory[6] and the earlier theory of relativity show that matter is in fact energy, which is consciousness in motion (or motion in consciousness). For energy is synonymous with motion and consciousness is the substratum, or deepest level, of all existence.

Now all motion arises in stillness, exists in stillness, is known by its comparison with stillness, and eventually subsides back into stillness. For example, if you walk across a room, before you start there is stillness, as you walk the room is still and you know you are moving relative to this stillness, and when you stop once again there is stillness. In the same way every 'thing' (consciousness in motion) arises in awareness (consciousness at rest), exists in awareness, is known in awareness and subsides back into awareness. Awareness is still, but is the container of all potential energy which is continually bubbling up into manifestation (physical energy) and then subsiding back into stillness.

Thus there is no dichotomy or duality between the physical world and 'awareness' for they are both manifestations of the same essence. The

---

[6] This posits that all 'things' are composed of 'strings' of energy in complex configurations, vibrating at various frequencies.

physical universe is just cosmic energy (consciousness in motion) when it is manifest into physical form, and awareness (consciousness at rest) contains this same energy in latent form as potential energy.

According to Vedanta philosophy this consciousness manifests into form purely for its own enjoyment and to experience itself as 'the many'. It manages this experience by awareness of every thought and sensation experienced by its many manifest forms. Thus our mind/bodies are instruments through which this universal consciousness senses, experiences, interacts with and enjoys its own manifestation: the physical universe.

If at this stage you can truly see that there exists a deeper level of 'pure awareness', that beyond the thoughts/sensations you are this awareness, and if you have experienced the peace of this recognition, then you may go on to Chapter 13, 'So What? ... What Now?' The following eight chapters of meditations and contemplations should be returned to for deepening your realization/recognition as and when you please. However, if you are still totally identified with your thoughts/sensations you should continue to the next chapter, or return to Chapter 2 and continue from there. At all events these meditation/contemplation chapters need to be treated as such, that is worked through slowly step by step until one 'sees' and 'feels' what they are pointing to. Alternatively one can go straight to Chapter 10, 'Relax into Self-Realization' which contains a very potent and simple test proving the existence of awareness; this chapter also emphasizes the importance of a totally relaxed approach in the investigation of experience.

Chapter Five

Nothing to Achieve, Find or Get

What follows is a discussion of the fact that there is nothing, which is external to ourselves, to be acquired. All that is needed is to realize the deeper level inherently present in each of us.

In terms of enlightenment, freedom, *moksha*, *nirvana* or liberation there is nothing to achieve, nothing to find and nothing to desire, long for, or acquire. All that is required is to recognize *what is* (already here), that which you already are, at a deeper level than body/mind (thoughts and sensations): awareness itself! Let us deal with these tendencies of the mind (to achieve, find, or acquire) in turn:

Nothing to achieve

It is impossible and needless to achieve what is already the case. There is already awareness of every thought, otherwise you would not know them and awareness of every sensation, otherwise you would not experience them. The mind is perceived as a flow of thoughts, and likewise the body is perceived as a flow of sensations; beyond these flows of ephemeral objects is the perceiver, the constant conscious subject, awareness itself. This subject is not a 'thing' but a field of subjectivity (consciousness) which encompasses all 'things'. This is already (and always) present otherwise we would not be conscious of our own thoughts and sensations. At a deeper level than this flow of fleeting objects (thoughts and sensations) we are this constant subject, awareness itself; this is already the case and as such cannot be achieved. All that is required is to realize this!

Nothing to find

It is impossible to find awareness as it cannot be lost, only overlooked, and so all that is required is to stop overlooking what is already here. Even while you are thinking such thoughts as 'I haven't got it' or 'I've lost it' you are aware of these thoughts, which proves quite categorically that awareness is present. This simple awareness of thoughts and sensations is all that we are talking about here, and the fact that you are aware of your thoughts and sensations proves that it is always present. Descartes described it as 'this internal awareness of one's thoughts and existence, which precedes reflective knowledge, and is innate in all men'.[7] Describing it as 'internal' is very apt for all objects are 'external', whilst the awareness of them is the 'internal' subject. One could say that our bodies/minds, which we perceive as flows of fleeting objects (thoughts/sensations), exist on the periphery of our being whilst at a deeper level we are the perceiver, awareness itself, which exists at the centre of our being. So awareness is central to our being, whilst thoughts and sensations are peripheral. This is self-evident for without awareness our thoughts and sensations would pass unnoticed. Thus we cannot lose this awareness; we just need to stop overlooking it.

---

[7] J. Cottingham, *Meditations on a First Philosophy*, 1996, Cambridge, p. 69

Nothing to get

It is impossible to get that awareness which you already are, and thus have in full abundance. All that is required is to recognize this. In this respect you do need to 'get' this, but this is in fact nothing as it is not a thing but the 'ground' from which all things arise, in which they exist and back into which they subside. So there is in fact 'no thing to get' and you do need to 'get' nothing(ness)!

To sum this up very simply: there is nothing to achieve as there is awareness of this thought (that there is nothing to achieve). Therefore awareness is already present and need not be achieved. There is nothing to find as there is awareness of this thought (that there is nothing to find). Therefore awareness is already present and need not be searched for. There is nothing to acquire (or get) as there is awareness of this thought (that there is nothing to acquire). Therefore awareness is already present and need not be acquired or longed for.

Enlightenment *is* identification with this awareness. To show how identification with this awareness manifests as awakening, freedom, enlightenment, *moksha*, *nirvana* or liberation, it is necessary to investigate awareness itself, and discover that it is:

> Effortlessly and choicelessly present, and effortlessly and choicelessly aware of all thoughts and sensations occurring in it.

Absolutely still, aware of the slightest movement of body or mind. In fact awareness is consciousness when it is completely at rest, aware of all movements that are occurring within it.

Totally silent, aware of the slightest sound or thought occurring within it.

Utterly at peace, for to be absolutely still and totally silent is to be utterly at peace.

Omnipresent, for all things (manifestations of cosmic energy) are forms of consciousness in movement, and thus arise in awareness, as all movement arises in stillness.

Omniscient, for all things exist in it, and are 'known' by it, just as all movement exists in a substratum of stillness and is known by (comparison to) that stillness.

Omnipotent, for all things subside back into it, just as all movement subsides back into stillness; and no thing has power over it.

Thus awareness is truly the source from which (and in which) all things arise, that in which all things exist and are known, and that into which all things subside. This is also:

> Pure, for no thing can taint or affect it in any way.

> Pristine, for no thing can degrade it.

> Radiant, for it illuminates everything that appears in it.

> Limitless, for it contains and encompasses all things.

So now we have reached the 'Pure, radiant, still, silent, omnipresent, omniscient, ocean of effortless, choiceless, awareness' (the Absolute) which, at the deepest level, we all are. Give up all striving, seeking and desiring, and identify with This which, at the centre, you already are. Identification with This, the constant centre, rather than with the periphery, the mind/body gives instant peace, for awareness is always 'still and silent' totally unaffected by whatever appears in it.

Chapter Six

On 'This' and 'That'

Here is a simple poem which sums up all we have discovered so far and adds a few pointers to what is to follow.

On This and That

Don't freak…
You are what you seek!

Let go of all anxiety for you are, at the deepest level, pure awareness, the realization of which is the enlightenment you are seeking.

Forget about church…
Just give up the search!

Abandon all dogma, belief systems and rituals, just stop the search (outward and inward) and relax into the pure awareness which you already are, without which you would be unaware of any thoughts or sensations.

No need for a prayer mat...
Already you are That!

No need to appeal to any external or internal deity for already you are That: pure awareness, just turn your attention to this.

No me, No you!
There's nothing to do...

In reality there is no separate individual entity (me or you). We are both just different expressions of the same pure awareness, and there's nothing we need do to awaken as we are already 'That'.

Nobody, No mind!
There's nothing to find...

At the deepest level there is nobody (separate individual) and no entity called the mind, which is just a flow of ephemeral thoughts. There is also nothing to find in that we cannot lose that pure awareness that, at the deepest level, we always are.

No effort, No sweat!
There's nothing to get...

There is no need to make any effort to achieve enlightenment; just stop and turn your attention to that pure awareness that you already are. You cannot 'get' this as you already 'are' this!

Wow! There's only Now…

In reality there is always only now as the past has already gone and the future is yet to be. If you see 'what is' in the 'now' with no reference to past, including acquired knowledge, or future then everything seems much more vivid and alive (Wow!) than when filtered through the mind and its opinions, judgements, attitudes and knowledge.

Cheer! There's only Here…

You are always here at any given moment, and can only see 'what is' here (and now). What you think is going on anywhere else is only speculation which will take you away from the direct experience of 'here and now'.

How? Just Here and Now!

How to be 'enlightened', i.e. unburdened and at peace? Just be totally here in the present moment and see 'what is' (here and now) with no reference to the past, future or what might be happening anywhere else.

Just This! That's Bliss...

This seeing 'what is' with a still mind from pure awareness is bliss. A Hindu name for The Absolute is *Satchitananda* which can be translated as: *Sat* - 'what is', *chit* - the awareness of 'what is', *ananda* - the bliss of the awareness of 'what is'.

Just Cease! That's Peace...

Just cease all of your mind activity to get anywhere, find anything or attain anything, and the result is instant peace.

Just Being! That's Freeing...

Just 'being' moment-to-moment, with no reference to any illusory separate self, is in itself totally freeing.

> Accept it all…
> Then have a ball!

Always accept 'what is' at the present moment with no resistance and life becomes enjoyable as the mind stills. This does not mean that we cannot plan to change things, only that we need to accept 'what is now' as it is already here and cannot be changed.

> Each moment is enough…
> The end of all (mind) stuff!

If you check you will find that pure awareness never needs anything to change and is complete whatever is happening. In this 'each moment is enough' and no mind activity is necessary to change, or seek for, anything.

> See 'what is' with no story…
> Then all reveals its glory!

If you see 'what is' with no story about it, or reference to past or future, then everything in manifestation appears more vivid and alive.

Chapter Seven

Nothing Special

This chapter points to the fact that awareness is so commonplace, always present, as to be 'nothing special'. However, this should not mask the fact that this presence is of paramount importance; as it is the source, existence and dissolution of all manifestation.

Recently, in commenting on an earlier chapter, somebody described awareness as 'nothing special' as if they were disappointed by this. There are two different interpretations of 'nothing special' (noting that the phrase contains only one negative) which will be considered in turn:

1. 'Something of no importance' (OED, Oxford English Dictionary) or something which is not 'better, greater, or otherwise different from what is usual' (OED). Whilst it is true that awareness is not 'different from what is usual' it can be argued that it is 'greater' than any thing, and is certainly of great importance. The first thing to note is that awareness is not an object but the 'constant, conscious, field of subjectivity'. This is certainly not 'different from what is usual', for being always present it is completely usual ('habitually occurring', OED). As this is the 'field' in which all things arise, exist and subside, then this is certainly greater than any thing, and is of greater importance than any thing.

2. 'Not anything' which is 'better, greater, or otherwise different from what is usual' (OED). This is almost correct in that awareness is not any thing, and is better, greater and different than any thing; although as shown previously it is 'usual'. It is different in the sense that awareness denotes consciousness totally at rest, aware of all movement occurring within it, whilst any thing is just a movement occurring in consciousness itself. Therefore awareness is better and greater than any ephemeral thing, being the 'ground' in which every thing arises, exists

and subsides.

So, allowing for some reservations, the definition of awareness as being 'nothing special' can be said to be fairly accurate. Also from a common-sense point of view awareness is unexceptional, in the same sense that the air we breathe is unexceptional, for it is always present and we could not exist without it. However, the fact that oxygen exists in the atmosphere, at breathable levels, is exceptional compared to any other planet we know, which makes it even more exceptional than awareness itself. For without the substratum of awareness (consciousness at rest) nothing would exist at all! This implies that the definition of 'nothing special' (in a universal sense) only applies to awareness itself, that which is 'not any thing', and 'habitually occurring'.

To illustrate the ordinariness of this awareness consider the following from *The Tibetan Book of the Dead*:

> This radiant and lucid awareness is itself referred to as 'ordinary consciousness',
> On account of those periods when it abides in its natural state in an ordinary way.
> However many pleasant-sounding names are applied to this awareness,
> Those who maintain that these do not refer to this present conscious awareness,

> But to something else, above and beyond it,
> Resemble someone who has already found an elephant,
> But is out looking for its tracks (elsewhere).[8]

This is why recognition of ourselves as pure awareness feels like 'coming home', for awareness is always present and the 'home' from which we stray when we identify with the mind, body or indeed as any 'thing' at all. Indeed our *home is where the heart is*; not a physical location but the 'central, innermost' (OED) essence of everything.

The problem is that enlightenment, freedom, *moksha*, liberation, *nirvana*, call it what you will, has been described in such glowing terms that we expect it to be an ecstatic, unforgettable experience. Whereas the realization, that at a deeper level than mind/body one is awareness itself, may seem so obvious as to be 'nothing special'. The consequences of this realization may lead to ecstatic experiences, but these should not be confused with the realization itself. However, if this realization is 'cultivated' so that one becomes completely identified with awareness itself, then this is enlightenment, freedom, *moksha*, liberation, *nirvana*.

---

[8] Padmassambhava, *The Tibetan Book of the Dead*, translated by Gyurme Dorje, 2006, London, p. 51

Chapter Eight

Home Is Where the Heart Is

Pointing to the fact that our true home, which can never be left, is the heart (central, innermost and vital part) of our being. This is where we feel totally at ease, peaceful and carefree.

To be truly 'at home' in the universe is to be totally free from all existential angst and anxiety, to be utterly at peace, to feel absolutely free to be what one is, to feel completely accepted and loved, with no judgement whatsoever. One of the best definitions of such a 'home' is in the Oxford English Dictionary: 'a place where something flourishes or from which it originated'. Another definition is: 'the place where one lives'; which gives the clue to being totally 'at home', for if one could truly 'live' in the 'place in which one originated and where one flourishes' then the problem would be solved.

This may be all very well but where is such a place and how do we find it? Here that old saying 'home is where the heart is' gives the clue; not the physical heart but 'the central. innermost, and vital part' (OED) of our being. Also 'where the heart is' symbolises that which we love and where we are totally loved and accepted. All that needs to be determined now is: where is the 'central, innermost, vital' level of our being, where there is absolute oneness; in which all things arise, exist and subside? For in *this* all things are loved and accepted as they are never separate from *this*.

This is pure consciousness which has two different modes or levels: firstly, when it is totally still, at rest, aware of everything that is occurring within it (that is pure awareness); to be totally aware of what is going on in a busy environment one has to be still, just witnessing the activity. Secondly, when it is in motion (cosmic energy) manifesting as the physical universe; for the string theory, and the theory of relativity, both show that matter is synonymous with energy. Now all motion arises in and from stillness, exists in stillness, is known by its comparison to stillness and finally subsides back into stillness. For example, when a train is at the station it is still, as it travels the terrain it traverses is still and you know it is moving relative to this (still terrain), and when it stops at the next station once again there is stillness. Therefore every thing, which is a manifestation of cosmic energy (consciousness in motion), arises in awareness (consciousness at rest) exists in awareness, is known by awareness and finally subsides back into awareness.

Thus our true essence, from whence we originate and where we flourish, is this level of awareness, where there is only peace and tranquillity, being the level of consciousness that is totally still and at rest. This awareness is always present as we are always aware of our thoughts and sensations, which in themselves are manifestations of cosmic energy. These are ephemeral arising in, existing in and returning to awareness, the constant, conscious, subjective presence; which at the deepest level we truly are.

This is the substratum of existence, the most fundamental and essential level of being; for even at the level of manifestation we could not exist without awareness of our thoughts and sensations.

This is our true 'home' where there is only 'oneness' (consciousness), and thus everything (just a movement in *this*) is loved and accepted as one with *this*. So to be truly 'at home' all we have to do is identify with (and as) this pure awareness, and see thoughts and sensations (indeed all physical objects) as what they truly are, ephemeral movements in *this*; which is easy to see just by taking a few moments to notice how thoughts and sensations, come and go in awareness, leaving it totally unaffected.

All that is needed to be 'where the heart is' (and thus totally 'at home') is to live in, and from, this 'central, innermost, vital' level of our being, which is awareness itself. For *this* is truly where we originate, in which we exist, to which we return, and that which we truly are. In *this* we are absolutely 'at home', totally free from all existential angst and anxiety, utterly at peace, free to be what one is, completely accepted and loved, with no judgement whatsoever.

Chapter Nine

Nothing Matters

A discussion of the different meanings of 'Nothing Matters' which shows how we can take 'things' less seriously. This chapter also highlights the vital importance of the nothingness that is consciousness at rest (awareness) and introduces the concept of relativity between 'things' and nothingness, in that we only become aware of any thing in contrast to the nothingness in which it exists.

An earlier chapter posited that awareness can be described as 'nothing special'. This is a companion piece considering the idea that 'nothing matters'. There are three different interpretations of 'nothing matters' which will be considered in turn:

No thing matters

There is no 'thing' in existence that truly 'matters', i.e. is 'important or significant' (OED). Now this judgement is usually made on a subjective basis, but this is not what we are considering here, as there are obviously things which seem important to individual minds. What we are considering is whether any 'thing' has significance, or importance, in absolute terms. As all 'things' are ephemeral, appearing and disappearing, coming and going, rising and falling, in the absolute field of consciousness and energy, leaving this field unaffected in itself, then no-thing can have any lasting significance or importance. Thus 'no thing matters' in absolute, or cosmic, terms.

Even at the seemingly personal subjective level we let the every-day minutiae of life matter much more than it should, allowing it to fill our minds, overlaying the peace of the deeper level of awareness. As autumn leaves settling on the surface of a pond obscure the calm waters beneath, we allow the smallest things to dominate our thoughts thus preventing us from seeing life as it truly is.

Nothing matters

That is to say that 'nothing' is, in itself, of great significance or importance. The 'nothing' that we are talking about here is the field of consciousness at rest (awareness), which is the 'no-thing-ness' that is the source, existence, knower and dissolution of all 'things' (manifestations of consciousness in motion). Thus it can be readily seen that this 'no-thing-ness' is of great importance and significance as no 'thing' could possibly exist without it!

The 'standard model' of the universe that is presently overwhelmingly favoured by astronomers and physicists is one of manifest matter/energy, 'dark matter' and 'dark energy'. In this model 'matter/energy' accounts for only a small percentage of the universe, whilst 'dark matter' is required to create enough gravity for the galaxies to hold together the way they do, and 'dark energy' is needed to account for the measured rate of expansion of the universe. Computer models have shown that the universe cannot manifest in the way it does unless 'dark energy' accounts for at least 50 per cent, 'dark matter' for at least 25 per cent, and 'matter/energy' the remainder. Many scientists posit that detectable matter/energy accounts for less than 5 per cent of the total!

Unfortunately, this 'dark matter and energy' is totally undetectable as it is not manifest, i.e. unmanifest, that is to say that it is 'no-thing', but even from the point of view of our universe (the manifest) it is of great significance and importance, as without it our universe would not exist in its present form.

Nothing 'matters'

Nothing is 'mattering', that is producing 'matter'. Isn't English a wonderful language! This is particularly apt, for as has already been pointed out: matter which consists of cosmic energy (consciousness in motion, or motion in consciousness), arises from this aware nothingness (consciousness at rest), exists in this, is known by this and finally returns back to this. For all motion arises in stillness, exists in a substratum of stillness and eventually returns back into stillness. Therefore this 'aware nothingness' does produce 'matter'.

Also at the personal subjective level this 'nothingness' is vitally important, for all 'things' are known or seen or perceived by their contrast with 'nothingness':

> There is awareness of all thoughts relative to the silence (no thought) in which they appear, exist and subside.

> There is awareness of all bodily feelings relative to the neutrality (lack of feeling) in which they appear, exist and subside.

> There is awareness of all sounds relative to the silence in which they appear, exist and subside.

There is awareness of all forms (things seen) relative to the space (formlessness) in which they appear, exist and subside.

There is awareness of all odours relative to the odourlessness in which they appear, exist and subside.

There is awareness of all flavours (tastes) relative to the neutrality (lack of flavour) in which they appear, exist and subside.

As the only things in our direct experience are thoughts (including all mental images) and sensations, awareness of which is only possible due to contrast with the 'nothingness' in which they appear, then this 'nothingness' is absolutely vital for awareness of any 'thing', and is in fact a property of awareness itself.

As has been previously shown, this awareness is the substratum in which all 'things' arise, exist, are known and subside. When we identify with this deepest level of our being, rather than the surface level of thought/sensation (body/mind), we can see that not only does 'nothing matter', but also that at this deepest level 'no thing matters'.

Chapter Ten

Relax into Self-Realization

This chapter highlights the importance of relaxation, letting go, in assisting self-realization. Also contains a simple test to check the presence of awareness, whilst reiterating that what is being referred to is the natural awareness of our thoughts and sensations.

The simplest and easiest way to realize one's essential nature is to *totally relax* into pure awareness, which is the deepest, most fundamental level of one's being.

At this suggestion the mind is likely to say, 'How do I do this?' or 'How can I find this state of relaxation?' or 'How can I get there?'

This is easily solved by realizing that there is nothing to achieve, for awareness is already present; there is nothing to find, for awareness cannot be lost; and there is nothing to get, for you already have and are awareness.

If you doubt this, apply the following simple test: ask yourself the question 'Am I aware of my thoughts and sensations?' If the answer is 'yes' then awareness is already present, and if 'no' then you are dead! Even in sleep there is awareness of dreams, the quality of the sleep and sensations; for if the sensation becomes strong enough it will wake you up. It is actually impossible to answer 'no' to this question as you can't ask/answer questions when you are dead, and you can't answer any question without being aware of the question itself! Therefore this proves that awareness is present.

Assuming that you have answered 'yes', all that you need now is to see that thoughts and sensations are ephemeral objects which appear, exist and are seen, then disappear back into awareness which is the constant subject. Just take a moment and notice how thoughts and sensations come and go, whilst awareness is a constant presence.

Awareness is like the screen on which all of our thoughts and sensations appear, and the mind becomes conscious (or sees) these by focusing on them or turning its attention to them. In fact, apart from deep sleep, the mind is always looking at this screen, for it is here that it collects its data to process. Although this is the case, it tends to focus on this data (thoughts and sensations) whilst not noticing the screen on which they are seen.

The mind, which is experienced as a flow of thoughts, and the body, which is experienced as a flow of sensations, are both flows of ephemeral objects. This does not mean that at a surface level we are not the mind and body, for they arise, are perceived and subside back into awareness which is the deepest and most fundamental level of our being.

Now you can relax completely letting go of all effort, searching, desiring or acquiring, confident in the recognition that deeper than body/mind you are this ever-present awareness. This field of subjectivity is akin to the 'cosmic audience' (of one!) that is viewing the movie of the universe and the lives of everything within it.

As you relax more deeply into this pure ocean of awareness and identify with it as the deepest level of your being, realize that we are always floating in, and as, an ocean of utter peace. For awareness is always absolutely still and totally silent, which implies that it is always in a state of perfect peace; for absolute stillness and total silence *is* perfect peace. This peace is always present no matter how turbulent things may be at the peripheral levels of mind and body, and may always be immediately accessed by relaxing back into that pure, pristine, radiant awareness that we are. There is absolutely nothing in existence that can disturb this peace, for all things rise and fall in this ocean of peace, leaving it totally undisturbed. Just relax and check it out!

Chapter Eleven

Mantra as a Vehicle of Revelation

This chapter is for those who need a method or 'practice', in addition to the direct recognition of pure awareness.

Although there is nothing to achieve, find, or get (as that which we are, at the deepest level, pure awareness is always already present), we need to recognize and be mindful of this in order to live in such a state of effortlessness. For example, if one has inherited vast wealth there would be no need to work for a living, but this is only the case if we are aware of our inheritance. If we fail to recognize or forget this we may well find ourselves struggling to gain that which we already possess. This is exactly the case of the person who has not recognized or has forgotten their spiritual inheritance: pure awareness, the substratum of all existence.

This is where realization and then remembrance, which is stressed by all mystical traditions, is especially useful to combat forgetting our true nature and losing ourselves in materiality. One method of doing this is mantra repetition, which can be an amazingly powerful tool provided that it is done alertly within the correct frame of reference. My favourite mantra is '*Om Nama (h) Sivaya*', the mental repetition of which has four major components:

The 'internal sound' and its vibrations

When repeated mentally the mantra sets up an internal 'vibrational field' which, it is posited, is very beneficial both physically and spiritually. If repeated with enough mental concentration this can also still the mind which can reveal the 'nothingness' behind all manifestation. However, this requires a supreme effort of will which can take many years to achieve. This is what is relied upon by meditators who are unaware of, or do not consider important, the following components:

The meanings

Om represents Brahman, The Impersonal Absolute, Logos, The Word, and the Ground of Being, in which all manifestation arises, exists and subsides.

Nama means 'name', and is almost certainly the root from which the word 'name' is derived. *Namah* means 'salutations' (to).

Sivaya, (of) Siva which is the 'total Godhead', the 'Supreme Reality'. Siva represents universal consciousness when it is at rest, aware of every movement occurring in it, which is pure awareness. Everything in manifestation is a form of cosmic energy (Sakti), which in itself is movement in consciousness. Energy is synonymous with movement and consciousness is the substratum in which all manifestation arises, exists and subsides.

So one reading of the mantra is that the Absolute Reality, Brahman, is (the name of) 'Consciousness at rest; pure awareness'; or 'salutations to the Absolute Reality which is pure awareness'. Another is that *Om* is the sound which represents (is the name of) Brahman, The Absolute, pure awareness. As such *Om* may be used as a mantra in its own right. This is backed up by the *Mandukya Upanishad* which says that Brahman may be realized by 'stilling the mind… and meditating on the mantra *Om* which stands for the supreme state of *Turiya* [superconsciousness or pure awareness], without parts, beyond birth and death, symbol of everlasting joy. Those who know *Om* as the Self become the Self; truly they become the Self' (*Mandukya* v.11-12).

The awareness of the mantra repetition

As one repeats the mantra, there is effortless and choiceless awareness of this repetition. This very awareness is, in itself, that which the mantra is addressing. By recognition of this, one can see that the mantra directly points to that which it is extolling: pure awareness. If one remains mindful of this, whilst repeating the mantra, then the 'revelation' has taken place. Alternatively, repetition of the mantra immediately reminds one of this pure awareness, our true 'spiritual inheritance'.

The 'nothingness' in which the mantra arises, exists, is 'known' and subsides

This is the 'nothingness' which can be revealed by repeating the mantra with intense concentration, thus blocking out all other 'things' from the mind. However this nothingness may be immediately realized by seeing that every 'thing' appears in nothingness, exists in nothingness, is known relative to this nothingness and disappears back into nothingness. Without this background of nothingness there would not be awareness of any 'thing'. As the only things in our direct experience are thoughts (including all mental images) and sensations, awareness of which is only possible due to contrast with the 'nothingness' in which they appear, then this 'nothingness' is absolutely vital for awareness of any 'thing'; and is in fact a property of awareness itself. 'Consciousness at rest' implies the 'subjective field' which is conscious (aware) and still, that is 'nothingness' as all 'things' are forms of cosmic energy, and thus in motion.

So if one repeats the mantra (or any mantra) noticing the awareness of the repetition and the nothingness (no thought) in which it arises, exists and subsides, then the mantra has done its job in revealing the nature of reality. In fact every single thing in manifestation points directly to this 'aware nothingness', or 'formless awareness', in exactly the same way. For it is in contrast to the nothingness that any thing is perceived, and awareness is that which underlies perception, in that one is effortlessly and choicelessly aware of sense (and mind) perceptions. However, mantra repetition has the added advantage of pointing to this directly by its form and meaning, for every mantra extols different aspects of this Absolute Reality. This 'aware nothingness', or 'formless awareness', is Jehovah, God the Father, Allah, Brahman, Siva, The Void (Theravadan Buddhism), Rigpa (Tibetan Buddhism), Big Mind (Zen), and The Tao. Mystics of all persuasions who follow the 'negative path' have come to this same realization of the Absolute Reality, although they give it different names.

Chapter Twelve

Every Thought, Each Sensation, Directly Reveals Reality

Building upon the previous discussion of relativity, nothingness and awareness, this chapter shows how everything we perceive can point us to the nature of the Absolute Reality.

Every Thought, Each Sensation, Directly Reveals Reality

If viewed in a certain way, everything that we perceive, that is, every thought and sensation can directly reveal the nature of Reality. For there are two underlying principles that lie at the heart of each perception, without which it would be impossible for any perception to occur. These are awareness and nothingness, for we would not know that a perception has occurred without being aware of it, and perception of any 'thing' only occurs relative to the nothingness in which it occurs.

When we look at any form (thing) we see this form in contrast to the space that surrounds it, without which we would not be able to see it. Consider a marble statue sculpted from a single block of stone. The statue only appears as the stone is chipped away, leaving the space that envelops the form. Before the sculptor begins, the form already potentially exists in the block of stone, but this only becomes apparent when the space in which it exists is exposed. Similarly *all* sensations are only known in contrast to the nothingness in which they occur and appear. Sounds, for example, are only known (heard) relative to the silence that surrounds them. If there is no silence, then either the sound is not heard, or it is muffled or distorted. For instance, if a bird is singing at 40 decibels and a lawn mower is being operated at 80 decibels you will not hear the bird. As soon as the mower is switched off the bird song is immediately heard within the silence that envelops it.

It is obvious that we would not 'know' (be aware of) our own perceptions without awareness being present. This does not mean that we are always conscious of each one of them, as this is dictated by where we place our attention, or upon what we focus our mind. However, all sensations detected by the body are there in awareness, and we can readily become conscious of them by turning our attention to and focusing the mind upon them. It is also true of our thoughts and mental images that they immediately appear in awareness; but these require less attention or focus to be seen as they occur in the mind. Thoughts are also perceived in contrast to the silence (no thought) in which they occur; if there is too much noise, either externally or in the mind, we tend to say 'it's too noisy to think straight'.

Now nothingness implies stillness, for all 'things' are manifestations of cosmic energy (quantum physics and the string theory affirm this), and therefore in motion. Even if they do not appear to be in motion, at the atomic level there is the constant motion of electrons orbiting the atomic nucleus. Therefore where there is total stillness, nothing could exist. It is posited that the Absolute Reality is consciousness at rest, aware of every movement that occurs within it. All motion arises in stillness, exists in stillness, is known by its comparison with stillness, and eventually subsides back into stillness. For example, if you walk across a room, before you start there is stillness; as you walk, the room is still and you know you are moving relative to this stillness; and when you stop once again there is stillness. In the same way every 'thing' (movement in consciousness) arises in consciousness at rest (The

Absolute Reality), exists in consciousness at rest, is known relative to this stillness, and subsides back into consciousness at rest.

So the two properties of this Absolute Reality are consciousness, that is awareness, and stillness which implies nothingness. Therefore every sensation or thought, which requires awareness and nothingness to be known, can be seen to directly reveal this Absolute Reality.

Chapter Thirteen

Nothing to Do, No Problem to Solve

Here it is shown how the recognition of this ever-present awareness can still the mind, and how committing to this recognition may prevent the mind from following thoughts and sensations as they arise and subside.

If you sit quietly, noticing that awareness is always present, it is very easy to see that for this to be the case there is absolutely nothing that the mind needs to do. Similarly there is no problem that the mind needs to solve to recognize this deeper level of awareness, as this very awareness is never absent, being the constant conscious presence in which all thoughts and sensations appear. For without this presence we would not be aware of any thought or sensation.

The mind is basically a problem-solving device, so when it realizes that there is nothing it needs to do and no problem that it needs to solve, it naturally quietens leaving the cloudless sky of awareness in its full glory. Provided one has the intent of identifying with this deeper level of awareness, then thoughts and sensations appear as clouds in this sky, which come and go leaving the sky unaffected. In this context the mind will not follow or identify with these clouds, as the task it has set itself to perform is to identify with awareness itself.

To reiterate: the mind is akin to an onboard computer, which is a wonderful tool for problem-solving, information storing, retrieval and processing, and evaluating the data provided by our senses. However, when it is not 'engaged' it tends to search for other problems to solve, and if these are not available in the present moment it tends to speculate about the future, wallow in the past, or imagine in the present, creating non-existent problems which it then tries to solve. Whereas, a computer will just sit idle until it is given a task to perform, so to put the mind into this same idle state one firstly has to 'engage' it in a task thus disabling its 'search' tendency. Then when it turns out that this task entails no problem to solve, the mind will not resume searching as long as it remains totally engaged in the task it has been set, and if this entails 'nothing to do' then the mind may just 'do nothing'! If it turns out that your mind continues to demand activity, it can be set the task of investigating the nature of the ever-present awareness that we all are.

In this mode, thoughts and sensations come and go effortlessly, without luring the mind to follow or identify with them. This is why committing or having the intent to identify with the deeper level of our being - pure awareness - is so important; for this sets the 'milieu' in which the mind is to operate. This in turn leads to the realization that for this identification there is truly nothing the mind has to do, no problems to solve, as awareness is obviously already here and is a constant presence (the perceiver) whilst thoughts and sensations are just ephemeral objects (the perceived).

At this moment you can totally relax, letting go of all striving, seeking, desiring and longing, all effort. As this relaxation deepens and the mind stills, one becomes totally open to further revelations stemming from the recognition that one *is* pure awareness. For this reason the *intent* to identify with this deepest level of our being, and the *realization* that for this there is truly nothing the mind needs to do or problem it has to solve, are of great value in going totally beyond identification with the surface level of thoughts and sensations.

This total relaxation and letting go then effortlessly leads to sinking deeply into awareness itself, with all the peace and bliss that this entails. For in this state there is truly 'no mind', as the mind is still, having nothing to do and no problem to solve; thoughts and sensations are merely witnessed as they spontaneously arise and subside, without reactivation of the mind.

Chapter Fourteen

So What? ... What Now?

This chapter considers how to apply recognising the deeper level of awareness to living in the day to day world and highlights the benefits of this recognition.

So What? ... What Now?

If you have got this far you will, I hope, have experienced the peace provided by truly knowing that beyond the mind/body there is a deeper level of pure awareness. However, you could say 'So what?' for we have to live in a body in the physical world with all of its associated problems. The trick here is to learn to live from this deeper level of awareness whilst negotiating living in the world. This has five major components, the first of which is primary, and if completely adhered to takes care of the following four:

1. Be committed to completely identifying with the deeper level of pure awareness, for in this there is always perfect peace and repose. Before this complete identification with pure awareness is established one will flip/flop between identifying with awareness and identifying with a mind/body. Awakening is an ongoing process with complete identification with pure awareness as the final goal. For it is in fact a series of awakenings, which is very necessary due to our natural tendency to go back to sleep! Every time we 'flop' back to identifying ourselves as mind/body we have nodded off again; and so the 'flip' to identifying with the deeper level of our being is another awakening. The author knows this only too well, and makes no claim to 'lack of sleep'. As one investigates and cultivates this deeper level, the periods of 'wakefulness' are prolonged and consequently one 'nods off' less. The period of time between one's first awakening and being completely awake is indeterminate and varies greatly from being to being. However, this is not a problem, for as the periods of 'wakefulness' (which are totally carefree) increase so will the commitment to

identifying with the level of pure awareness. This will lead to more reflection and investigation, resulting in further awakenings which will continue the process. To call it a process may seem a misnomer for when one is 'awake' there's no process going on, but the continual naps keep the whole thing running.

This commitment to identifying with the level of pure awareness involves having faith in our body/mind to negotiate living in the world, for this is what it has evolved to do. This 'complete identification' will not happen all at once but is something that has to be cultivated. I would recommend doing this by spending three periods of at least twenty minutes, every day, totally relaxing into the recognition of pure awareness. The best times for this are between getting up and engaging in one's daily activities, after the day's work is over and just before going to sleep. The first 'sets one up' for the day, the second refreshes and re-energises one after the day's toil, and the third aids in achieving a deep and peaceful night's sleep. One may argue that there is not enough time available for this, but these meditations provide so much relaxation and recharging that one can easily recover the time by sleeping for an hour less.

When meditating/contemplating, the body needs to be completely at ease, so pick the most comfortable position you can find. For instance, the final session can be carried out lying flat on your back just before dropping off to sleep. There should be no distractions, but if there are any just notice them as ephemeral objects that come and go in the constant conscious subjective presence that underlies all thought and sensations. You may use any of the preceding eleven chapters as aids to your relaxation and investigation into the recognition of pure awareness. As time goes by you will make your own discoveries and verbalize your own pathways into this recognition. I strongly advise you to record in writing these discoveries and pathways, as the reading of them before your practice will put you in the right frame of mind, and inspire you. In the final analysis your 'pathway in' will become particular to your own mind, and writings produced by your mind will always appeal more than those produced by another mind. Ultimately you have to become, as the Buddha said, 'a light unto yourself'.

2. To avoid identifying with your thoughts and mental states, you need to stay alert so that you are not carried away by negative (or any) mind-states. For a stream of thoughts and mind-states continues to come up whatever your degree of realization; however, as complete identification with pure awareness is cultivated, this stream will diminish. The point is to recognize these thoughts and mind-states for what they are: ephemeral objects which come and go quite naturally, leaving the constant conscious subject untouched. It is important not to identify with them (as mine or me) and thus give them extra weight. To avoid this, practice treating them as entertainment and either thank the mind for bringing them up, or examine them as strange phenomena. As your realization deepens, this will happen spontaneously and no effort will be required.

So What? ... What Now?

3. Learn to trust the mind/body. The body functions quite naturally without much mental intervention being necessary. We do need to feed and clothe it, but apart from that it functions quite happily, provided we are alert to the signals that it emits such as hunger, thirst, tiredness, inertia, etc. As far as solving the problems involved in living in the physical world are concerned, we have at our disposal the most amazing instrument, the human mind, our own inbuilt onboard computer. As previously said, this is a wonderful problem solving device, but to function properly it needs to be supplied with accurate data. All computer errors are due to incorrect data or program bugs. The main program bug in the mind occurs when we identify ourselves as the mind. In this case it colours all of the data it receives with its own opinions, judgements, self-interests and so on, which naturally leads to erroneous conclusions. As we learn to identify with the deeper level of pure awareness, this bug is fixed, and we learn to see things 'as they are', rather than through the filter of the mind. Now data is fed in uncontaminated, and problem-solving activity continues more accurately and spontaneously.

4. Accept 'what is' with no resistance, for resisting what is here and now only causes suffering. Such thoughts as 'I wish this wasn't the case' or 'If only... then this wouldn't have happened' cannot possibly change what is 'here and now', and only lead to dissatisfaction and anxiety. If such thoughts do come just let them come and go without buying into them, by either regarding them as entertainment or thanking the mind for them. This does not mean that we cannot or should not

plan to change things in the future for the better or so that we do not find our selves in the same situation again. It is self-evident, however, that we are powerless to change 'what is' as it already is!

This also means accepting our mistakes and not berating ourselves for them, for until we are totally identified with, and as, pure awareness, we will continue to make mistakes. Normal life is a mixture of correct decisions and mistakes and should be accepted as such. As we become more 'awake' we will make less mistakes, but until then we can always see any annoyance caused by our errors for what it is: just a mixture of fleeting thoughts and sensations. Once again, if one relaxes into the deeper level of pure awareness one will see that this is totally unaffected by anything occurring at the surface level of mind/body. At this deeper level each moment is enough, or perfect in itself, as awareness just witnesses 'what is' without ever seeking to change anything.

5. Live totally in the present moment with no regard to the past or future. This naturally occurs once one begins to live by following the previous components. Then thoughts about the past and future will be seen for what they are, ephemeral objects which come and go. Also the stream of thoughts and mental states will decrease and thus the mind will experience longer periods of stillness. When this occurs one sees things 'as they are' in reality, and this combined with acceptance of 'what is' leads to the mind's preferences and judgements losing their power. This does not mean that you will have no preferences, but that

you will remain unaffected if they are not satisfied. One of the easiest ways to bring oneself into the present moment is to completely focus on the bodily sensations and see them as they are with no judgement and without reading any non-specific meaning into them.

One of the major pitfalls of the mind is to read meaning into things that have no meaning. All superstition and much of religion is based on this, and when this occurs it takes one away from experiencing what is 'here and now'. This is a classic case of the mind creating imaginary problems which it then attempts to solve. At first one will find that present moment awareness is only a fleeting state that comes and goes, but the more you completely identify with pure awareness the more this state comes, and remains, and the less it goes.

When there is this complete identification (merging with awareness) one discovers that it has many wonderful by-products, most of which are considered to be spiritual disciplines in the mystical paths of the world's religions. However, practising these disciplines to achieve self-realization is an example of putting the cart before the horse, for the recognition of oneself as pure awareness is primary and these disciplines are secondary outcomes of this. Some of these wonderful by-products are as follows:

Compassion

Once one sees that at the deepest level one is pure awareness, it follows that this is known to be the case for all sentient beings. At this level there is truly no separation between oneself and any other being, and this naturally leads to compassion.

Discrimination between the 'real' and the 'unreal'

This level of pure awareness is classified as the 'real'; it is constant, unchanging and unaffected by any 'thing', whereas the level of manifestation of things is classified as 'unreal', it is always changing and is governed by the laws of cause and effect. Once one becomes completely identified with pure awareness then this becomes obvious and no discrimination is needed.

Love of God and one's fellow man

The word God means consciousness having two states: at rest (pure awareness), and in motion (manifestation). In this there is truly no separation as the essence and ground of all that exists is consciousness, and true love is only present where there is no separation; true love is 'no separation'. The Christian idea that 'God is Love' points to this, and love of one's fellow man naturally follows from the realization of no separation.

Contentment and remaining unaffected by external circumstances

Pure awareness is always unaffected by external circumstances, thus complete identification with awareness naturally leads to this quality of being.

Detachment

Pure awareness is always complete in itself and prefers no 'thing' or circumstance, being the witness to these. Therefore detachment is its natural condition. This does not mean that we will have no preferences at the level of mind/body, just that we will remain unaffected if these are not fulfilled as there will be no attachment or clinging to them.

Therefore in this complete identification with pure awareness one is totally beyond the 'separate self', for even as it continues to rear its ugly head one does not buy into or identify with it. There is also no more existential anxiety or mind-induced suffering. This is not to say that mental and physical pain will not occur – these are an unavoidable facts of bodily existence – but they will not produce mental suffering for they will be seen for what they are, ephemeral states which come and go. Even in the case of prolonged physical pain it is possible to accept this without resistance, so that although there is pain this does not cause mental suffering. Also, in this complete identification one can always sink into the deeper level of pure awareness where there is only peace and tranquillity.

Chapter Fifteen

All or Nothing

A discussion about the importance of committing to identifying with the deeper level of awareness in going 'beyond the separate self'.

At this point you may say 'Well that's all very well but what about *me* and *my* story?' For it has long been held by Western psychology that the sum of one's experiences and conditioning makes up what one *is*. This may well be true at the surface level of mind/body, but not at the deeper level of pure awareness in which these experiences come and go leaving no lasting impression. It is the surface level that is the domain of the 'separate self', the ego, and this is where anxiety and mental suffering occurs.

At this stage one needs to come to a decision about which one values more: the objective level of thoughts/sensations or the deeper subjective peaceful level of pure awareness. If one chooses the former then life will just continue with its highs and lows, suffering and anxiety, and obsession with the 'separate self'. One will also continue to see everything through the distorting filter of the mind, its opinions, judgements and self-interest, which lessens one's perceptions as if seeing through a darkened window. However, if one chooses the latter then all perceptions are heightened by seeing things clearly, 'as they are', for when nature is seen 'as it is' it is much brighter, more vivid, more stunning than when seen through the mind's filter. So by identifying with pure awareness the objective level of sensations is enhanced, and thus becomes more valuable in its own right. This gives the lie to the idea that sinking into the deeper level of being means that one enjoys the world less; in fact the reverse is true!

It may be true that one can continue to value the surface level of thoughts/sensations more, and occasionally sink into the deeper level of pure awareness for a brief respite from the troubles of daily life. However this does not tap the full potential of identifying with, and as, this deeper level completely beyond the 'separate self', and experiencing things 'as they are' in their absolute immediacy and totality. In this mode there is no concern for the future, and the past completely loses its hold, thus all worrying comes to an end. For this to occur one has to completely let go of 'my story' and see everything in the past for what it is, totally gone and in the past.

This is truly a case of *all or nothing*, for once any exception is made then this is the thin end of the wedge as it sets a precedent for other past experiences to be held on to. It has to be completely realized that nothing that has happened in the past or will happen in the future can possibly affect the deeper level of pure awareness.

I have heard from many people who, having glimpsed this deeper level, continue to argue for the value of 'working through past experiences', and in this they are dishonouring that which they have glimpsed. For the only way that you can completely work through past experiences is to totally let them go, and not buy into them when they reoccur in the mind or body. They will continue to come up, but any attention that is lavished on them only feeds and strengthens them; when ignored they are starved of attention and their reoccurrences will slowly peter out. By 'ignored' this do not mean 'suppressed', for this will also strengthen them, but just allowed to 'come and go' with no weight being given to them. As soon as you start telling yourself a story about what they mean, or how they have affected you, you are back at the surface level of the 'separate self' and the ego. If the physical feelings are too strong to ignore they can be defused by going completely into them without any 'story', and noticing that they are just sensations which have arisen and will subside quite naturally. It is the telling of the story that prolongs them, feeds them and invites them to reoccur.

However, even these unpleasant memories/feelings point directly to pure awareness for this is where they occur and are noticed by the mind. This brings up a very important point: any time where there is any mental suffering caused by identifying with painful thoughts, or feelings, this should be a wake-up call to the fact that we are misidentifying. Any mental suffering can be used as a direct pointer back to the deeper level of our being: pure awareness.

So to fully tap the potential of this deeper level one needs to fully commit to identifying with, and as, this. This commitment is paramount, for, as previously pointed out, one will continue to flip/flop between identifying with the deeper and surface levels of our being. As we have spent so many years identifying with the mind/body, we will naturally tend to do this, so we need to continually bring our attention back to the deeper level and to commit to doing this.

In the final analysis the surface level is the abode of the 'separate self', ego, with all of its attendant self-obsession and suffering. The only way to go totally beyond this is to dive deeper than this and discover 'the peace that passeth all understanding' of pure awareness. This, however, will not totally inform and transform one's life until one totally commits and identifies with this.

Chapter Sixteen

The Full Potential

This chapter considers the potential of 'awakening', illustrating this by discussing the Bodhisattva Path of Mahayana Buddhism.

What is the full potential of completely 'waking up' and recognizing the deeper level of one's being; the constant conscious subjective presence that is pure awareness? This is actually impossible to define as the deeper you go the more is found, and the potential is literally boundless. What is being investigated is itself boundless. The great masters say that there is no end to awakening and spiritual experience, there's always more to be discovered - what a wonderful idea! You will find this is more than an idea, for you will discover that the deeper you go, the more you identify as this deeper level, the more that will be revealed.

We have already found that this leads to perfect peace, seeing things 'as they are', acceptance of 'what is' and living totally in the present moment. As one becomes more closely attuned to this realization by nodding off less frequently, and these 'properties' become more firmly established, then many further discoveries will take place. As an example we will consider the Mahayana Buddhist masters who have investigated this closely and have come up with a system of ten stages (*bhumis*), starting with the first awakening and ending with the final 'perfection', when one is constantly 'awake'. They call this the 'Bodhisattva Path'. A bodhisattva is defined as an awakened being who chooses to be reborn, time and time again, to help others 'awaken'. Note that they believe in reincarnation (about which we cannot know by direct investigation and this book expresses no opinions) which is central to their description of the ever deepening realization of the potential of 'awakening'.

On the realization of the deeper level of pure awareness, and the identification with this, one has reached the first stage (*bhumi*), that of joyfulness, where one proceeds by developing the six *paramitas* or perfections. Nagarjuna (the author of many of the early scriptures of Mahayana Buddhism) states that these are 'the perfections of *giving, morality, patience, vigour, meditation* and *wisdom*.'[9] Also at this level one has realized that there exists no separate individual being (object), for we all share the same constant conscious subjective presence that is pure awareness. This is central to Buddhism, a concept which they call *anatta*, which literally means 'no self'. The other central plank of Buddhism is 'impermanence', *anicca*, by which they simply mean that every 'thing' is impermanent. This is self-evident for any 'thing' is just a movement in consciousness, a manifestation of cosmic energy, and all movement eventually subsides back into stillness.

Chogyam Trungpa talks of *giving* in terms of generosity without any philosophical, merit-acquiring or religious motives. The aim is to give with an open heart with no judgement or evaluation of ourselves or those to whom we are giving. In the same way, being completely open and seeing 'what is' with no reference to 'self' then our actions are

---

[9] E. Conze, *Buddhist Scriptures*, 1959, Harmondsworth, p. 32

These 'perfections' are give in a special font so that the reader can track them as they occur in the following discussion of the *bhumis*.

always pure and *morality* is spontaneous. Similarly *patience* is natural to one who sees things 'as they are' and accepts 'what is' with no resistance. For in this state there is complete ease of being with nothing to strive for or attain and thus infinite patience. This lack of both resisting and striving liberates tremendous amounts of *vigour* which can be used to help others to go beyond suffering. This produces joy which itself liberates more energy which enhances the deepening of the awakening which has begun. This deepening produces a state of 'panoramic awareness' or constant *meditation* in daily life, so that action becomes *meditation* and vice versa. Finally this 'panoramic awareness' produces deeper *wisdom* by always seeing everything 'as it is' with no reference to an individual seer. This enhances the realization of the truths of *anatta*, no self, and *anicca*, the impermanence of everything. It also means that we respond spontaneously to life situations in a balanced way, rather than reacting to them from an egocentric point of view.[10] Thus once one has attained *bodhicitta* (enlightenment) and the 'awakening' has begun in earnest with the attendant selflessness (literally no self) and joyousness, then the developing or deepening of the *paramitas* (perfections) and attainment of the higher levels, or *bhumi*s, happens effortlessly and naturally, provided one does not re-identify with an 'individual self' or the ego. The fact that this may take many aeons is unproblematic as there is no resistance and no desire to achieve or attain anything. This produces a total state of 'living in the present' and 'seeing what is' in which time is totally irrelevant as each moment is enough, or perfect, in itself.

---

[10] Chogyam Trungpa, *Cutting Through Spiritual Materialism*, 1987, Boston, p170-178

To this list of six perfections some traditions add another four - skill in means, determination, strength, and knowledge - so that there is one *paramita* to correlate with each of the ten *bhumi*s. The perfection of these ten *paramitas* make up the 'path of the bodhisattva', culminating in the tenth level, 'the Cloud of *Dhamma*', and the attainment of 'full Buddhahood'.[11]

Now we will consider the stages themselves in detail starting with the 'joyful'. This stage is reached automatically once one has realized, and identified with, the deeper level of pure awareness. This creates great compassion and joy[12]: 'Governed by compassion to liberate living beings completely, and always abiding in joy is called the first' (1.4cd, 5ab).[13] One is now truly a bodhisattva and cannot fall back, provided one does not re-identify as an individual self:

> Because he has attained this, he is addressed by the very name Bodhisattva .... all paths to lower births have ceased .... all grounds of ordinary beings are exhausted (1.5cd, 7abc).[14]

During this stage one perfects generosity (*giving*) through helping others to overcome suffering. This occurs naturally and spontaneously out of compassion and seeing 'all as oneself'.

---

[11] R. Gethin, *The Foundations of Buddhism*, 1998, Oxford, p. 230

[12] All of the following scriptural quotes (i.e. those with chapter and verse numbers) come from the 'Guide to the Middle Way' by Chandrakirti, the principal disciple of Nagarjuna, which are contained in: G. K. Gyatso, *Ocean of Nectar*, 1995, London

[13] G. K. Gyatso, *Ocean of Nectar*, 1995, London, p. 38

[14] Ibid. p. 39

The second stage is called the 'stainless' and is attained by purity and moral discipline; this occurs naturally provided one lives in the realization of *anatta* (no self). If one re-identifies with an 'individual self' this can result in losing *bodhicitta* and committing impure acts which will lead to 'losing ground': 'If enjoyments that result from giving arise in a lower rebirth, it is because that being broke his legs of moral discipline' (2.4ab).[15] As Buddha said to Kashyapa:

> They (who propound a self) may appear to possess moral discipline but have faulty moral discipline ... They who abide in the apprehensions of 'I' and 'mine' may appear to possess moral discipline but have faulty moral discipline.[16]

Purity, or *morality*, is crucial to becoming a bodhisattva: 'Because his conduct of body, speech and mind is pure, he accumulates all ten paths of holy actions' (2.1cd).[17]

The third stage is called the 'luminous' in which one develops *patience* and forbearance thus overcoming anger. Once again selflessness is the key: 'Furthermore for the bodhisattva who has seen selflessness, what is cut [i.e. his body] by whom, at what time and in what manner - all these phenomena are seen to be like reflections. Therefore he is patient' (3.2).[18] To generate anger one must identify with a 'self' that is under attack,

---
[15] Ibid. p. 81
[16] Ibid. p. 80
[17] Ibid. p. 77
[18] Ibid. p. 91

either physically or mentally, whereas a bodhisattva has compassion for the bad karma created for and by the attacker. This ground is called 'luminous' for through the knowledge of no self, and thus emptiness, one experiences a luminous glow that pervades the whole environment on arising from meditation.

The fourth stage, the 'radiant', is where one perfects the use of energy, *vigour* or effort which arises spontaneously out of awakening. It should be noted here that the word effort here does not mean striving or strain but an almost effortless use of the energy, arising from spontaneity and joy, in perfecting giving, purity, patience and meditative concentration. This type of effort is praised: 'All good qualities follow upon effort, the cause of the two collections of merit and wisdom. The ground on which effort blazes is the fourth, Radiant' (4.1).[19] On completion of this stage one has finally completely overcome self-grasping and is totally and irrevocably grounded in *anatta* (no self): 'And what is related to the view of self is completely eradicated' (4.2d).[20]

The fifth stage is called 'Difficult to Overcome' for 'this great Being on the ground Difficult to Overcome cannot be defeated even by all the *maras*' (5.1ab).[21] For when there is no self-identification with the mind or body then all of the mind-created demons (*maras*) are seen for what they are and therefore have no power. Thus one can perfect the virtue of *meditation* as the distractions of the mind are seen for 'what they are'

---

[19] Ibid. p. 118
[20] Ibid. p. 125
[21] Ibid. p. 128

and so lose their power. Through the power of this *meditation* one realizes the 'Four Noble Truths' in all of their depth and profundity.

The sixth stage, 'approaching', or 'face to face', is noted by perfecting *wisdom* and gaining 'full insight into Conditioned Arising, not-self and emptiness'.[22] At this point the bodhisattva has reached the level of *arhatship* and could enter the final *nirvana,* i.e. not be reborn. However, having taken the 'Bodhisattva Vow' and being filled with compassion, this option is spurned so that the bodhisattva may continue to work for the good of all beings. Even whilst the bodhisattva is absorbed in thoughts of (or meditations on) 'emptiness' or 'cessation', he 'still generates compassion for protectorless living beings'. (6.225)[23]

The seventh stage, 'gone afar' is characterized by the ability to realize 'emptiness' instantaneously and the perfection of 'skilful means'. 'Here on Gone Afar, he can enter into cessation instant by instant. And he has also attained a surpassing perfection of means' (8.1).[24] At this stage the bodhisattva is beyond *karma* and rebirth and has become a heavenly being (*Maha-Sattva*) who can 'magically project himself into many worlds' so as help beings overcome suffering.[25]

The final three stages, 'immovable', 'good intelligence' and 'the cloud of *dhamma*', are known as the 'pure grounds' in which the final obscuration, that of the 'knowable', is overcome.[26] During these stages

---

[22] P. Harvey, *Buddhism*, 1990, Cambridge, p. 123
[23] G. K Gyatso, *Ocean of Nectar*, 1995, London, p. 384
[24] Ibid. p. 338
[25] P. Harvey, *Buddhism*. 1990, Cambridge, p. 124

the ultimate virtues and absolute purity are attained, *samsara* is overcome and the thirteen forces of the bodhisattva are perfected. Finally, 'On the tenth ground he receives holy empowerments from Buddhas in all directions, and he also attains a supreme surpassing exalted awareness. Just as rain falls from rain clouds, so for the sake of living beings ... a rain of *Dhamma* spontaneously falls from the Conqueror's son'(10.1).[27] With this full Buddhahood is achieved and the bodhisattva passes beyond the ten stages.

This is a very culturally informed view of the potential of 'awakening', but it does give a hint as to the possibilities that lie ahead as one deepens one's realization of and identification with the fundamental level of pure awareness. From a beginner's point of view it is encouraging to note that the first stage is joyful, and that this joy is totally independent of any external circumstances or things; but that this wells up from the recognition of oneself as pure awareness. As long as one does not re-identify as a separate object, at the surface level of mind-body, then this joy (or peace) is a constant presence, which may be overlooked but can be readily re-accessed by direct investigation. As has been already pointed out, as soon as any mental suffering occurs this should be a wake-up call that one is back identifying at the surface level of thoughts and sensations.

The wonderful point is that joy (or peace) *is* the first stage, and after that things only get better and better, as long as one increases one's

---

[26] P. Williams, *Buddhist Thought*, 2000, London, p. 180
[27] G .K. Gyatso, *Ocean of Nectar*, 1995, London, p. 399

identification with the deeper level of pure awareness. All suffering is at the surface objective level, and whilst bodily pain is common to all bodies, this does not cause suffering at the deeper subjective level of awareness. So once one has gone beyond the 'separate self' of identification as a separate object, in a universe of separate objects, then one has truly transcended all anxiety and suffering.

Chapter Seventeen

The Best of All Worlds, Humanity at Its Peak

This chapter suggests that humanity reaches its peak potential, in terms of acting humanely, by identifying with the deeper level of pure awareness. Also, the more of us who manage this the nearer we get, in terms of human interaction, to 'the best of all worlds'.

It could be argued that this book denies our humanity by stressing that which is 'beyond the separate self', i.e. beyond the mind/body. However, I would argue that identifying with the deeper level of our being, pure awareness, enhances our humanity immeasurably; and if this were the common condition then all instances of man's inhumanity to his (or her) fellow man would be consigned to history. For, as has been shown, this deeper identification leads to joy, peace, love of all beings (in fact of the whole of existence) and true selfless compassion. This is because at this level there is no separation as all of manifestation is seen to be just the play of consciousness, cosmic energy, movements in consciousness itself.

A study of the world's religions reveals two major themes concerning the purpose of creation and the function of humanity. It is suggested that the Absolute, consciousness at rest (pure awareness), created (or manifested as) the universe for Its enjoyment and so that It could know Itself. For when consciousness is totally at rest It has no objects to be aware of, and thus no form of experience is possible; so the only way for any enjoyment to occur is for the 'potential energy', latent in the Absolute, to manifest into cosmic energy and thus the universe. Then instruments are needed to 'sense' this manifestation, so that these sensations appear in awareness, which is the function of all conscious organisms.

As far as 'knowing Itself', It needs some form of mechanism, such as the human mind, which is capable of self-recognition; and this is what occurs when we realize our deeper level of being which is this pure awareness itself. For this realization appears in the mind and thus in awareness itself. Thus the human mind/body has the function of attaining self-realization and enjoying existence in order that the purpose of creation is fulfilled. This enjoyment of existence is greatly enhanced by seeing and experiencing the world 'as it is', that is by encountering it totally and directly rather than through the filter of the mind. This occurs only when we identify at the deeper level than body/mind so that the mind's opinions, judgements, interpretations, etc. are seen for what they are, ephemeral thoughts coming and going in awareness itself. As one deepens one's identification with pure awareness the mind stills and then the world is encountered directly, with 'no mind', and is experienced as it truly 'is'. A Hindu term for the Absolute is *Satchitananda*, which can be translated as: *Sat*-'what is' (the manifestation), c*hit*- the awareness of 'what is', *ananda*- the bliss of the awareness of 'what is'.

In fact once one relaxes into pure awareness one can actually feel the bliss of embodiment through the sensations in the body, a subtle throbbing of the life force, and through that which is detected by the other senses. This bliss is present in every moment and can be detected by bringing one's whole attention to the sensation in question, without any 'second thought' about the sensation and what it could mean or without relating it to any 'story' of oneself. This culminates into being totally in love with the whole of existence, a love where the beloved is always present as there is no separation between the lover and the beloved. The lover being the deeper level of pure awareness, consciousness at rest, and the beloved being the surface level of manifestation, consciousness in motion. In this context *Satchitananda* becomes: *Sat* –the beloved, *chit*- the lover beholding the beloved, *ananda* - the bliss of the lover beholding the beloved.

The corollary to this is that when one achieves self-realization, recognizing that at a deeper level one is pure awareness, then this is the beloved beholding the lover. The beloved being the surface level of mind/body, the manifestation, realizing the deeper level of consciousness at rest, the lover. This completes the cycle of the Absolute using the mind/body to sense, experience, interact with and enjoy its manifestation, and also to recognize (or 'know') Itself.

If one lives in this state of self-realization, and therefore no separation, joy is one's natural state, whilst love of one's fellow beings occurs spontaneously by the realization that they are of the same essence (as oneself) and equally valuable instruments of the Absolute. In this state all greed, cruelty, envy, lust for power, exploitation, hatred and mind created suffering (caused by identifying with the surface level of mind/body) cease completely. This revolutionizes our interactions with humanity at large, and if this were the common condition then there would be no more instances of man creating suffering for his fellow man.

This would truly be the best of all worlds for humanity, as we all seek joy and peace; the problem is in general that we look in the wrong place, the external world, rather than the centre of our own being. So to create this Utopia we need to commit to identifying with the deeper level of pure awareness, and to encourage those around us to do the same. The more we become established in this level of identification the closer we come to the peak of human existence and thus the more we enhance our true humanity.

Chapter Eighteen

Purpose and Meaning

This chapter discusses purpose and meaning, showing how identifying with our deeper level of pure awareness leads to enjoying life to the maximum.

In this chapter I shall discuss Hindu cosmology and its divine 'plan', although 'play' would be more appropriate. I shall then consider whether this makes life meaningful. I will attempt to show that when one engages totally in this 'play', life becomes so enjoyable and pleasurable that no other meaning or purpose is necessary. Finally, I shall consider some objections that could be raised for such a view and offer counters to them.

For me the most plausible divine plan/purpose rests in Hindu cosmology. In this, Brahman (the totality of cosmic power, energy, consciousness and awareness) rests as a single point before the creation of the universe. Compare this to the 'singularity' which modern physics/astronomy posits existed before the 'big bang'. From Brahman is manifested the universe and he pervades it, or dwells in it *as it*. In *The Gospel of Ramakrishna* we find:

> After the creation the primal power dwells in the universe itself. In the Vedas creation is likened to the spider and its web. The spider brings the web out of itself and then remains in it. God is the container of the universe and also what is contained in it.[28]

Brahman is considered to have two aspects, the male which is the witnessing/awareness aspect (consciousness at rest) and the female which is the aspect of creation, preservation and destruction (consciousness in motion). This manifestation of the universe occurred,

---

[28] S.Nikhilananda, *'The Gospel of Sri Ramakrishna'*, 1942, Chennai, p. 135

according to modern science, as the 'big bang'. The universe (manifestation) expands, continually evolving and growing until the energy (matter) becomes so 'spread out' that it returns to the aware nothingness (Brahman) from whence it came. For energy is (motion) vibration and as the waves are stretched the peaks/troughs become smaller and smaller until all returns to stillness.

This explains the cosmology, but what of plan or purpose? According to the Hindus this is all the 'play' of Brahman in the female aspect called the 'Divine Mother', which is purely for her enjoyment:

> The Divine Mother is always playful and sportive. The universe is her play. ... She wants to continue playing with her created beings. ... Her pleasure is in continuing the game.[29]

Before we can consider whether this makes our lives as a human beings meaningful, we have to consider what we really are. Are we just puppets who are being played with by some divine force, or manifestations of that force participating fully in the 'play'? According to the Hindus Brahman is 'the container of the universe and also what is contained in it'. Thus we are, in essence, also 'That' (Brahman) and able to participate fully in the 'play'.

However, this is not possible whist we consider ourselves as separate individual beings trying to make our way in an alien world. This is

---

[29] S.Nikhilananda, *'The Gospel of Sri Ramakrishna'*, 1942, Chennai, p. 136

mainly because this stops us 'being' the present moment and engaging totally in the 'play'. Consider the play of children who totally lose themselves in the game and thus participate fully with maximum enjoyment. As long as we consider ourselves to be a separate ego we are always trying to better ourselves, achieve more (knowledge, possessions, power, fame etc.), polish our self-image and generally build ourselves up. This tends to make us live in the future and stops us living fully in the present moment. The other side of this coin is to live in regret as to what might have been, self-loathing, melancholy or yearning for the past. This also stops us seeing 'what is' here and now, either by making us live in the past or by the mind spinning on our failures and lack of self-worth.

I realize that this goes against modern western thought which finds meaning in achievement/purpose rather than the sheer enjoyment of 'what is' at any given moment. Consider the following quotes from *The Meaning of Life*:

> What counts is that one should be able to begin a new task, a new castle, a new bubble.[30] (Richard Taylor)

> In so far as I have carved out my being in the human world, I go on existing in the future. [31] (Hazel Barnes)

---

[30] E. D. Klemke, *The Meaning of Life*, 2000, Oxford, p. 175
[31] Ibid. p. 166

I am not suggesting that having and achieving goals is not a source of great satisfaction, but it does not compare to the bliss evoked when one comes across a stunning sunset which is seen with a still mind, or when you are at a concert and you hear the music so deeply that you 'become' the music. This occurs when you totally 'lose yourself' in the manifestation. The point here is that the world is a wonderful place when seen 'as it is' with a still mind and no reference to a separate individual seer. In other words when it is seen in its actual reality and not through the narrow filter of the minds likes/dislikes, judgements and opinions. I can offer no proof of this apart from the fact that it is my experience and has also been pointed to by many mystics, past and present. This can, in fact, only be known *through* experience and not through reason and the intellect.

Why should this be the case? Our deeper level of pure awareness, an aspect of Brahman, is who we 'are' at a deeper level than mind/body. Our mind/bodies are the instruments with which It (as we) senses and 'plays in' Its creation. Thus when you filter any sensation through the mind you are 'colouring' it with something less (the mind's likes/dislikes, opinions and judgements) than the pure awareness in which it appears, and so masking its actual reality.

Finally, consider the problems that this view encounters. The first, and for the philosopher the main problem, is that it cannot be proved by argument and reason. In fact these are the tools which obscure it. It has to be experienced, but for this you have to know, existentially, that you are not separate from 'That', the totality of being. Unfortunately, this knowledge is impossible to obtain as long as you identify with the mind/body or as a separate individual. In this state one overlooks the pure joy and pleasure of living moment to moment and tends to feel that:

> Whenever we are…directed back to existence itself we are overtaken by its worthlessness and vanity and this is … called boredom.[32] (Schopenhauer)

This is because we are identifying with our rational mind and using it to judge every moment, rather than just 'being' with a still mind and experiencing the actual reality of existence.

Albert Camus unknowingly puts his finger on the exact problem when he says:

> Thinking of the future, establishing aims for oneself, having preferences … presupposes a belief in freedom. … But that freedom to 'be' which alone can serve as a basis for truth does not exist.[33]

The point is that pure 'being' can only be experienced when one is not 'thinking of the future, establishing aims and having preferences'; the two states are mutually exclusive, the second preventing the first!

---
[32] Ibid. p. 69
[33] Ibid. p. 99

Summing up: when one lives moment to moment, identified with the 'totality of being', one is able to engage fully in the 'Divine Play'. This makes life light, not heavy, and thoroughly enjoyable not requiring any extra meaning or purpose. It is only when identified as a separate individual, living in an alien world, that such meaning or purpose seems necessary.

Chapter Nineteen

The Absolute Reality

Here is a comparison of the Absolute Reality, pure awareness, consciousness at rest, with that posited by the world's five major religions. This chapter also attempts to show that each of these religions contains at least one mystical stream which reveals this same Absolute Reality.

The aim of this chapter is threefold: firstly, to show the fundamental differences and similarities in the way in which the major religions of the world conceive of God, the Absolute Reality or the Absolute Self; secondly, to compare these with the Absolute Reality that has been elucidated in the previous chapters; and thirdly, to show that, despite these differences, certain mystics from each of these religions have had very similar realizations (experiences and the knowledge they provide), although they may interpret these differently. These realizations could then be used to posit that the Godhead, or the Absolute, that each religion approaches, is in fact the same, just described in different historical and cultural language. Thus all religions are valid although they promulgate many different paths to reach the same goal. Therefore it can be argued that there are many different ways to reach the Absolute and each religion stresses various of these paths in its own way. As that mystical genius Sri Ramakrishna, who traversed many of these paths in a multitude of religions and experientially discovered that ultimately they led to the same realization,[34] said:

> God can be realized by all paths. All religions are true. The important thing is to reach the roof. You can climb up by stone stairs, wooden stairs, bamboo steps or by a rope.[35]

> Different people call on Him by different names; some as Allah, some as God, others as Krishna, Siva and Brahman.... Each

---

[34] S. Saradanand, *Sri Ramakrishna the Great Master*, 1978, Myalpore, p106-389
[35] S. Nikhilananda, *The Gospel of Sri Ramakrishna*, 1942, Chennai, p. 111-112

religion is only a path leading to God, as rivers come from different directions and ultimately become one in the ocean.[36]

The five major religions of the world will be considered, three from the Western traditions - Judaism, Christianity and Islam - and two from the Eastern traditions - Hinduism and Buddhism. In this chapter the term 'the Absolute (Reality or Self)' will often be used as this is an umbrella term for 'God', 'The Father', 'Allah', 'Brahman', 'Rigpa' and 'Universal Mind'. The ideas of the Absolute to be compared will be the fundamental, scriptural definitions as it is beyond the scope of this chapter to take into account the many later theological and sectarian opinions which have developed. Moreover, no consideration will be given to the worship of bodhisattvas (Buddhas in various stages of development who renounce *Nirvana* until all beings are liberated), *Avatars* (human incarnations of different aspects of the Absolute) or the pantheon of Hindu gods, all of which, it can be argued, are just different aspects of the Absolute.

Western Religions

In the Western tradition the religions of 'the book' will be compared in historical order: Judaism, Christianity and finally Islam. This is because the idea of the Absolute developed historically through the Old Testament, New Testament and the Qur'an, and because the followers of each later religion(s) accepted, up to a point, the scriptures of the

---

[36] Ibid. p. 264-265

former religion(s). It is interesting to note that the reverse is not true, in that the followers of the former religion(s) have not accepted the scriptures (or validity) of the later religion(s).

Judaism

In Judaism, the Absolute (God) is described as 'One' (Deuteronomy 6 v.4), revealing monotheism, but also as the 'God of Gods' (ibid. 10 v.17 and Daniel 2 v.47), 'judging among the Gods' (Psalms 82 v.1) and 'greater than all Gods' (Chronicles 2 v.5), indicating a belief by ancient Hebrews of a multitude of gods of whom God is the greatest.

The Absolute (God) is also described as 'Eternal' (Job 36 v.26 and Isaiah 57 v.15), 'The ruler of heaven' (Deuteronomy 10 v.14), 'All knowing' (2 Samuel 14 v.20), 'Holy' (Psalms 99 v.9 and others), 'In heaven' as compared to 'on earth' (Ecclesiastes 5 v.2) and 'On the high seat' or 'throne of holiness' (Psalms 47 v.8). These references highlight the transcendental, omniscient, omnipotent nature of the Absolute.

He is 'the Creator of heaven and earth' (Genesis Chapter 1), 'The King of all the earth' (Psalms 47 v.7), 'Ruler over Nations' (ibid. v.8), and the 'giver' of the promised land to the Israelites (Deuteronomy 19 v.1-3 and many more). Thus He is the creator and ruler of the earth and has singled out the Israelites as a 'chosen race' by 'giving' them the promised land.

He is also 'with you' (Joshua 1 v.9, Isaiah 8 v.8-10 and many more), 'Walking among you' (Deuteronomy 23 v.14), 'The rock of my heart' (Psalms 73 v.26), and in Job 27 v.3 it says 'The spirit of God is my life'. These point to the immanence of the Absolute who is always present.

He is not only present but 'Our safe place' (Psalms 62 v.8), 'my helper' (Isaiah 50 v.7), 'their strength' (Job 12 v.13 and many more), our 'protector' (Proverbs 30 v.5), 'teacher' (Isaiah 28 v.26) and 'salvation' (Jeremiah 3 v.23 and Psalms 68 v.20). Thus not only is He immanent but He also intervenes to help us, if we deserve it.

As well as helping man He also is a 'judge, angry with evil-doers (Psalms 7 v.11 and 75 v.7) whilst at the same time He is 'upright' (Daniel 9 v.14) and 'full of grace and mercy' (2 Chronicles 30 v.9).

There is some debate as to whether He was thought to be anthropomorphic for whilst it says in Genesis 1 v.27 that He 'created man in his own image' it also says that He 'is not a man or the son of a man' (Numbers 23 v.19). It would appear that while this does not mean that He is anthropomorphic in form, it was used to highlight man's special status above that of all other created beings. It also 'emphasises the continuity of God's being with man's being, projecting God as a more powerful more moral man-like entity. God emerges as personal, caring about man and needing to be placated by man'.[37]

---

[37] A. Unterman, *'The Jews'*, 1981, Boston, p. 20

So whilst the Absolute is transcendent, omnipotent, omniscient and eternal, He is also immanent and intervenes to help or punish us as we deserve. Not only that but He is personal with a (super) man-like nature with whom we can and should build a personal relationship.

Christianity

The Christian descriptions of the Absolute in the New Testament naturally have much in common with those in the Old Testament. God is described as 'One' (Mark 12 v.29, Galations 3 v.20), 'Omniscient' (1 John 3 v.20), 'The Witness' (1 John 5 v.7-9, Romans 1 v.9), 'All Powerful' (1 John 5 v.4), 'Never been seen' or ineffable (John 1 v.18) and 'Spirit' (John 4 v.24). Thus God is transcendent, omnipotent, omniscient, omnipresent, ineffable spirit. In contrast to the Old Testament there are no references to other gods.

Also God is 'in us' (1 John 4 v.12 and many others) 'among you' (Luke 17 v.21), 'all-giving (2 Corinthians 9 v.8), 'salvation' (Acts 28 v.28) and 'all-seeing' (Hebrews 4 v.12-14). So He is immanent in the world and the help and salvation of the just.

God is the 'true judge' (Romans 2 v.2), 'the ruler and giver' (Romans 11 v.22), 'good and merciful' (ibid.), 'wrathful' (Revelations 15 v.1) and 'hates pride' (1 Peter 5 v.5). These highlight that we are accountable to God for our thoughts and actions.

Other attributes of God are that He is 'love' (1 John 4 v.8), our 'Father' (John 14 v.6 and many more), 'light' (1 John 1 v.5) and an 'all burning (consuming) fire' (Hebrews 12 v.29). So God is our Father, full of light and love, in whom all pride, ego, and ignorance are consumed.

This leaves the central basic difference between Judaism and Christianity, the incarnation of God as man, and the doctrine of the 'Holy Trinity'. This is a great mystery which is not completely clarified by the scriptures. In John we find 'In the beginning was the Word ... and the Word was God ... And the Word was made flesh and dwelt among us' (John 1 v.1 and v.14). This shows that Christ is God 'made flesh'. Then in the same chapter is written:

> And John bare record saying: I saw the Spirit descending from heaven like a dove, and it abode upon him. And he said unto me, 'Upon whom thou shalt see the Spirit descending, and remaining on him, the same is he which baptiseth with the Holy Ghost.' And I saw, and have record that this is the Son of God. (John 1 v.32-34).

This tends to indicate that the 'Spirit' or 'Holy Ghost' is that aspect of the Absolute which manifests in the world and 'descends' on man. However, it is not clear why this should happen to Christ if he was already 'God made flesh'. Then in Luke 12 v.10 we find 'And whosoever shall speak a word against the Son of man, it shall be forgiven him; but unto him that blasphemeth against the Holy Ghost it shall not be forgiven.' This indicates some degree of separation between Christ, God made flesh, and the Holy Ghost, God as Spirit. Although John (20 v.22) records that Christ had the power to bestow the Holy Ghost: 'And when he said this he breathed on them, and saith unto them, Receive ye the Holy Ghost'. Mark also records some degree of difference between Christ (the Son) and the Absolute (the Father): 'But of that day and hour knoweth no man, ... neither the Son, but the Father' (13 v.32). Yet this is contradicted by Matthew when he says: 'And Jesus came and spake unto them saying, All power is given unto me in heaven and in earth. Go therefore and teach all nations, baptising them in the name of the Father, and of the Son, and of the Holy Ghost' (28 v.18-20). This seems to indicate three different entities and yet it is clear that this is not the case ('and these three are one', 1 John 5 v.7-10). Summing up, it appears that 'the Father', 'Holy Ghost' and 'Christ' are different aspects of 'The One (Absolute)' but that Christ was somewhat subject to the restrictions of being 'made flesh'.

Islam

The first thing to be said about Islam is that the Qur'an makes it quite clear that Allah is 'not the messiah, son of Mary' (Q V.17 and 72). Islam has great regard for Jesus as a prophet, but does not believe that he was the son of God: 'The Messiah, Jesus son of Mary, was only a messenger of Allah ... Far is it removed from his Transcendental

Majesty that He should have a son. Allah is only One God' (Q IV. 171).

As Islam basically accepts the Old Testament and the Gospels, whilst asserting that the Qur'an is the latest and final revelation which corrects errors in the former, it is not surprising that Allah, the Absolute, is described in very similar ways as God is in the Bible. Allah is 'all powerful' (Q II.109 and many others), 'all hearing and all knowing' (Q II.181 and many), 'everlasting' (Q XX.73), 'the truth' (Q XXXI.30), the 'only One God' (Q II.163 and many) and 'independent of all the worlds' (Q III.97). So the Absolute is omnipotent, omniscient, eternal, One and transcendent.

He is 'the creator of everything' (Q XIII.16), 'the lighter of the heavens and the earth' (Q XXIV.35), 'the king of the heavens and the earth' (Q V.17-18), and 'all things belong to him' (Q IV.131 and many). Thus he is the creator, ruler and owner of all of manifestation.

Also He is 'between the man and his own heart' (Q VIII.24), 'among/with you' (Q XLVII.35 and many), 'the seer of what they do' (Q II.96 and many) and 'able to send a sign' (Q VI.37). Therefore Allah is immanent, aware of man's thoughts and deeds, and able to respond to them.

He helps the just and believers by being 'bountiful' (Q II.251 and many), their 'guardian/protector' (Q II.257 and many), their 'embracer and knower' (Q II.268 and many), 'helper' (Q IV.45), 'guide' (Q XXII.16 and many), 'patient' (Q VIII.46 and many) and 'sufficient for you' (Q VIII.62 and many). So, for the believer, Allah provides everything that is needed and, in material lack, He alone is 'sufficient'.

Allah is also the judge of mankind being 'firm and punishing' (Q II.211 and many), 'swift in reckoning' (Q III.19 and many), 'mighty and vengeful' (Q III.4 and many) counterbalanced by being 'merciful and bounteous' (Q II. 105 and many), 'gentle and merciful' (Q II.143 and many), 'forgiving and merciful' (Q II.173 and many), and 'never unjust to his worshippers' (Q III.182).

Other properties assigned to Allah are those of being 'rich' (Q IV.131 and many), 'True in speech' (Q IV.122), 'my worshipful Lord' (Q III.51), 'the sender of the winds' (Q XXXV.9), 'high, great' (Q IV.34) and the 'enemy of the unbelievers' (Q II.98).

Allah, as so described, is very similar to the God of Judaism, and also that of 'The Father' of the Christian trinity. This is not surprising as all three religions developed from the same root, and all of their 'fundamental' descendants claim to belong to the lineage of Abraham.

Summing up the concept of the Absolute in the Western religions 'of the book', He is described as transcendent, eternal, omnipotent, omniscient, omnipresent, creator of everything, immanent, seer of all we do, aid and helper whilst judging our thoughts and actions. Although transcendent He is personal having many human-like qualities, whilst being our aid and judge, and thus can be approached by prayer, worship and devotion.

Eastern Religions

With regard to the Eastern religions Hinduism, more precisely Vedanta, will be considered first as this pre-dates Buddhism, which it influenced. Within the latter we will consider Theravadan, Tibetan and Zen Buddhism.

Hinduism

Hinduism is not in fact one religion but a vast variety of paths leading to liberation (or 'God realization') which evolved on the Indian sub-continent from the ancient Vedic religion of Brahmanism. These were based on the Vedas, a collection of scriptures written between about 1500 and 500 BCE.[38] It is beyond the scope of this chapter to consider all of these paths as they developed vastly differing views of God, or the Absolute, so we will concentrate on the Absolute as defined in the Upanishads which represent 'the last works of the Vedas, the final stage of Vedic evolution ... where the emphasis is away from ritual towards the personal and mystical experiencing of the One'.[39] The classical

---
[38] J. Hinnells, *Living Religions*, 1997, London, p. 264
[39] Ibid. p. 266

path, based on these books, is Advaita-Vedanta, Advaita meaning 'non-dual' and Vedanta being 'the end of the Vedas'. Thus Advaita-Vedanta, hereafter called Vedanta, is a form of 'non-dualism' based on the books at 'the end of the Vedas', which are the Upanishads.

In the Upanishads the Absolute, Brahman, is the source and creator of all manifestation (i.e. all universes) but also *is* everything within that manifestation:
1. 'Before the world was created the Self (Brahman) alone existed; nothing whatever stirred. Then the Self thought: "Let me create the world".
2. He brought forth all the worlds out of himself

Aitareya Upanishad (from the *Rig-Veda*) Part 1, Ch.1 v.1-2.

Not only is Brahman the universe, its origin and cause, but eventually all will 'return' to him: Not only is Brahman the universe, its origin and cause, but eventually all will 'return' to him: 'This universe comes forth from Brahman and will return to Brahman, verily all is Brahman' (*Chandogya* III 14.1). So from Brahman (consciousness) everything (all cosmic energy, consciousness in motion) exploded into being at the big bang, arising from the infinite potential energy already existing in This. Cosmic energy, manifesting as the universe, is continually evolving, rearranging and expanding at an ever increasing rate. As this occurs this will finally dissipate as each vibration (motion) finally 'runs out of steam' and returns to the consciousness at rest from whence it came.

As Brahman is everything, it follows that we all are Brahman and that He is the agent by which the mind thinks, eye sees, tongue speaks, ear hears and body breathes (*Kena* I v.5-9). He is also described as the 'ear of the ear, eye of the eye, mind of the mind, word of the words and life of the life' (*Kena* I v.2). Thus He is the 'pure awareness' (*Brihadaranyaka* 4 v.7) in which all thought, life and sensation appears; and He is the 'seer' (*Isha* v.8) and 'all knowing' (*Katha* 2 v.18). He is also described as 'one' (*Isha* v.4), 'radiant, everywhere, transcendent, indivisible, pure' (v.8). As the cause, existence and dissolution of everything that exists, He is 'immortal, eternal, immutable' (*Katha* 2 v.18), 'without beginning or end, beyond time and space' (3 v.15), 'infinite, imperishable and unborn' (*Mundaka* II 1.1 & 1.2). Although He is 'within all' *(Isha* v.5) and 'the light of man' (*Brihadaranyaka* IV v.6) He is also 'unseeable, ineffable and unknowable' (*Kena* v.3). This is because He is 'pure consciousness' (*Aitareya* ch.3 v.1) and the 'attributeless reality' (*Svetasvara* ch. 3 v.1). Thus all attributes appear in, exist in and disappear back into Brahman, but having no attributes He is unperceivable by the mind and the senses. Thus this 'pure awareness', Brahman, is the substratum and essence of all of existence.[40]

Buddhism

Buddhism has often been described as atheistic for the Buddha did not talk about the Absolute and refused to answer questions on the subject,

---

[40] E. Easwaran, *The Upanishads*, 1988, Penguin, New Delhi

instead maintaining a noble silence. This does not necessarily mean that the Buddha denied the existence of an Absolute Reality, but he did deny the existence of an individual self. It appears that he felt that the *atman* (Brahman within each individual) doctrine of Vedanta had been corrupted to the concept of an individual soul (or Self) which exists eternally. So to affirm the existence of the Absolute could have been construed as supporting this doctrine of (individual) 'eternalism'; but to deny the existence of the Absolute would have supported the doctrine of 'annihilationism' which would have contradicted the Buddha's own doctrine of *nirvana* (liberation), and thus he chose to remain silent.[41] However, he is said to have made the following inspired utterance about *nirvana* itself:

> There is, monks, a domain where there is no earth, no water, no wind, no sphere of infinite space, no sphere of neither awareness nor non-awareness; there is not this world, there is not another world, there is no sun or moon. I do not call this coming or going, nor standing, nor dying, nor being reborn; it is without support, without occurrence, without object. Just this is the end of suffering.[42]

This indicates some greater 'reality' which is attained when *nirvana* is reached, but it is described in a totally 'negative' way as being free of all attributes. As Buddhism developed and spread, this idea evolved into the Tibetan (Buddhist) concept of Rigpa or 'Ground Luminosity'

---

[41] R.Gethin, *The Foundations of Buddhis'*, 1998, Oxford, p. 161
[42] R. Gethin, *Udana 80* in *The Foundations of Buddhism*, 1998, Oxford, p. 76-77

and the Zen idea of 'Universal Mind'. Both of these concepts are equivalent to the 'pure consciousness' or 'awareness' in which all appears, exists and disappears. About Rigpa, Sogyal Rinpoche says, 'In Tibetan we call it Rigpa, a primordial, pure, pristine awareness that is at once intelligent, cognizant, radiant and always awake .... It is in fact the nature of everything'.[43] Dudjon Rinpoche adds, 'It has never been born, been liberated, been deluded, existed, been nonexistent, it has no limits and falls into no category'.[44] Padmasambhava, the founder of Tibetan Buddhism in 775AD,[45] described Rigpa as:

> The self-originated Clear Light which ... was never born. It has never experienced birth and nothing could cause it to die ... although it is evidently visible, yet there is no one who sees it ... Although it exists in everyone everywhere it has gone unrecognized.[46]

According to *The Tibetan Book of the Dead* Rigpa is the first thing one encounters after death: 'The nature of everything is open, empty and naked like the sky, luminous emptiness without centre or circumference; the pure naked Rigpa dawns'.[47]

Universal or Big Mind is the name used by the Zen school whose 'founding genius was seen as the semi-legendary Indian monk

---

[43] S. Rinpoche *The Tibetan Book of Living and Dying*, 1992, San Francisco, p. 47
[44] Ibid. p. 49
[45] P. Harvey, *Buddhism*, 1990, Cambridge, p. 145
[46] S. Rinpoche *The Tibetan Book of Living and Dying*, 1992, San Francisco, p. 260
[47] Ibid. p. 259

Bodhidharma ... active in China between 470 to 520 AD'.[48] About this 'Mind' he is recorded as saying:

> Only the wise know this Mind, this Mind called *dharma* nature, this Mind called liberation. Neither life nor death can restrain this Mind. Nothing can. It's also called the unstoppable *Tagatha*, the Incomprehensible, the Sacred Self, the Immortal, the Great Sage ... The Mind's capacity is limitless and its manifestations are inexhaustible ... The Mind has no form and its awareness no limit.[49]

We find this Zen Mind also described in *'Zen Mind, Beginner's Mind'* by Shunryu Suzuki as something which is 'always with you', 'watching mind' and 'our true Buddha nature'. He also talks about small 'I' and big 'I' and our 'true self'. Finally, he says, 'You should be able to appreciate things as an expression of big Mind '. [50]

Thus the Theravada School, which sticks to Buddha's original teachings, remain quiet on the existence or non-existence of the Absolute but does admit a supra-mundane state of *nirvana*, whilst the Mahayana schools of Tibetan and Zen Buddhism do accept an Absolute reality whose nature is of pure awareness or consciousness.

---

[48] P. Harvey, *'Buddhism'*, 1990, Cambridge, p. 153
[49] S. Rajneesh, *'Bodhidharma'*, 1987, Cologne, p. 71-72
[50] S. Suzuki, 'Zen Mind, Beginners' Mind', 1970, New York, p. 134-137

To sum up, the Eastern religions regard the Absolute as impersonal, unborn, ineffable, eternal, omnipresent, omniscient, omnipotent, infinite and yet within us all. Vedanta says that 'we are That' (Brahman), Tibetan Buddhism says that it 'exists in everyone everywhere', and Zen says that it is 'our true nature'. Moreover, Vedanta says that Brahman created the universe out of Himself, Tibetan Buddhism says that the Absolute is 'the nature of everything', whilst Zen Buddhism say that big Mind's 'manifestations are inexhaustible' and that 'things are an expression of big Mind'. These tend to indicate that not only is the Absolute the origin of everything, but that all things in manifestation are (different aspects of) the Absolute.

Comparison

The major differences between these Western and Eastern ideas of the Absolute are that the former are dualistic regarding the Absolute as personal and separate (from its creation, although in it), whilst the latter are monistic, viewing the Absolute as impersonal and not separate from its creation. This Western view is that God has human-like qualities and thus we can build a relationship with Him through prayer and devotion. In this way He will 'save us', 'protect us', 'help us' and generally look after us. However, although God is immanent and 'in us', He is forever separate in that we are not and cannot be 'That'. The Eastern view is that the Absolute is impersonal and yet not separate from us, or any of its creation. Thus we can realize that we are 'Brahman', 'pure awareness', Rigpa or 'big Mind', by following the various paths of liberation prescribed by the scriptures. This is not to say that there are not personal paths in the Eastern religions through the worships of *avatars*, bodhisattva*s*, or lesser 'gods', but that beyond these lies the impersonal Absolute in which these all arise, exist and subside.

The properties of the Absolute (awareness) that we have discovered during the meditation/contemplation chapters are:

>Omnipresence, for all things (manifestations of cosmic energy) are forms of consciousness in movement, and thus arise in awareness, as all movement arises in stillness.

>Omniscience, for all things exist in it, and are 'known' by it, just as all movement exists in a substratum of stillness and are known by (comparison to) that stillness.

>Omnipotence, for all things subside back into it, just as all movement subsides back into stillness; and no 'thing' has any power over it.

Thus awareness is truly the source from which (and in which) all things arise, that in which all things exist and are known, and that into which all things subside. This is also:

>Pure, for no thing can taint it, or affect it in any way.

Pristine, for no thing can degrade it.

Radiant, for it illuminates everything that appears in it.

Limitless, for it contains and encompasses all things.

Attributeless, for all attributes are ephemeral objects coming and going in it.

These can be seen to include all of the properties posited by the Eastern religions, and by the Western religions, with the exception of the personal aspect of the Godhead. However as *This* (pure awareness) is what we all are at the deeper level than body/mind, and we all have different minds and personalities, we therefore express and manifest *This* in different ways. Also as our mind/bodies are never separate from *This* but arise in *This*, exist in *This* and subside back into *This*, then *This* does indeed contain personal aspects. It's just that these are ephemeral and therefore not properties of *This*.

Mysticism

When considering mystical experience or knowledge of the Absolute, given the similarities of the way that it is viewed, it is not surprising that similar realizations should occur to mystics of the different religions. This is especially true of the so-called 'negative way' where everything that could be attributed to or said about the Absolute is stripped away, leaving the pure indescribable essence (or non-essence!). That this should be the case should not surprise us if we believe that the Absolute at the core of all religions is the same. For it is the trappings, properties and attributes assigned to this Absolute that are the product of the historical and cultural traditions that spawned the world's religions. So it is easier to show the similarities of experiences on the 'negative way' rather than on the 'positive way' in which these trappings, properties and attributes become the focus of attention. For example, a worshipper of Christ may attain a vision of Christ, but will never attain a vision of Krishna, whereas a worshipper of Krishna may attain a vision of Krishna but never of Christ. However, a Christian mystic and a Vaishnavan mystic may reach the same 'negative experience' of the Absolute through and beyond the worship of Christ or Krishna. So this chapter will concentrate on these negative experiences and the realizations they produce, as there is nothing to be gained from highlighting the differences between the various 'positive experiences', visions or revelations which are highly coloured by the religious view of the experiencer.

These 'negative' experiences are called 'introvertive mystical experiences' by W. T. Stace, which he sums up as follows:

> Suppose that, after having got rid of all sensations one should go on to exclude from consciousness all sensuous images, thoughts, reasoning processes and other particular mental contents; what then would there be left of consciousness? There

> would be no mental content whatever, a complete emptiness, vacuum, void. One would suppose that ... one would fall asleep or become unconscious. However the introvertive mystics – thousands of them all over the world, unanimously assert that ... what happens is quite different ... what emerges is a state of pure consciousness – pure in the sense that it is not the consciousness of any empirical content. It has no content except itself.[51]

This has often been described as 'nothingness' in that there is 'no thing', there is only pure awareness (consciousness at rest), the source, receptacle and dissolution of all 'things'. Or to put it another way, all 'things' arise in, exist in and subside back into this 'no-thingness'. Just as all forms appear in space, exist in space (and are known by their contrast to space), and finally return back into space; all sounds appear in silence, exist in silence (and are known by their contrast to silence) and finally return back into silence; and so on.

This 'nothingness' is found in Judaism in the medieval Kabbalistic concept of *ayin* (nothingness) from which 'everything emerges ... and eventually returns there'.[52] About this David ben Abraham La-Lavan, a fourteenth century Kabbalist says: 'Nothingness is more existent than all the being of the world but since it is simple, and all simple things are complex compared with its simplicity, it is called *ayin*.'[53]

---

[51] R. Forman, *The problem of pure consciousness*, 1990, New York, p. 106-107
[52] Ibid. p. 121
[53] Ibid. p. 122

The classic way of approaching this 'nothingness' is by stripping away (negating) all of the attributes and properties that have been assigned to the Absolute to reveal its pure essence. Maimonides the great medieval Jewish theologian promoted this method:

> Know that the description of God ... by means of negations is the correct description ... You come nearer to the apprehension of Him, may He be exalted, with every increase in the negations regarding Him.[54]

The Kabbalists called the Absolute *Ein Sof* (or *En-Sof*) which literally means infinite. From this emanate the *Sefirot*, the stages of divine being and aspects of divine personality. Thus a 'distinction is made between God as He is in Himself, the *En-Sof*, which is unknowable and impersonal, and the personal God of the Torah (the *Sefirot*) who is God in manifestation'.[55] This *Ein Sof* is hidden in the depths of nothingness and has no qualities or attributes.

The 'negative way' (*via negativa*) has been one of the two planks (the other being the *via positiva*) of Christian mysticism since being championed by Dionysius the Areopagite circa 500AD. Michael Cox maintains that it is 'the dominant path in Christian Mysticism' in which God, the transcendent and 'unknowable' can be approached only by stripping away every aspect and attribute assigned to God and the self.[56]

---

[54] Ibid. p. 127
[55] W. T. Stace, *Mysticism and Philosophy*, 1961, London, p. 177-178

For Dionysius, and all mystics on the negative path, God is the 'Hidden Dark', the Cause beyond all causes, the Origin of all and the 'unknowable'. About this he said:

> God is neither sonship, nor fatherhood nor anything else known ... He has neither darkness, nor light, nor truth nor error; ... we can neither affirm nor deny Him; for the perfect and sole cause of all is above all affirmation and subtraction, absolutely separate and beyond all that is.[57]

Meister Eckhart, that great Christian mystic of the thirteenth century, said of his discoveries on the negative way:

> God in the Godhead is spiritual substance, so elemental that we can say nothing about it excepting that it is naught. To say it is aught were more lying than true. His simple nature is in form formless, in mode modeless, cause uncaused, being without becoming which transcends all things becoming and all that becomes to an end therein.[58]

The other way of using the negative path is to strip away all attributes or properties of the seeming 'self' to reveal its source or essence. If God is truly immanent, with us and within us, then this method should reveal the Absolute at the centre of our being. It is this approach that is more

---

[56] M.Cox, *Christian Mysticism*, 1986, Great Britain, p. 34
[57] Ibid. p. 76
[58] F. C. Happold, *Mysticism*, 1963, Harmondsworth, p. 271

suited to Islam for the very word means 'submission', and in total submission there is self-abnegation. This is shown in the Sufi doctrine of *fana* 'absorption into Deity, the state of Reality, the "uncreated" world of mystery'[59] which al-Junaid of Baghdad interpreted as 'dying to self'. This leads to unification as Abu Hamid al-Ghazali explained:

> Now, when this state prevails it is called in relation to whom who experiences it, Extinction, nay, Extinction of Extinction, for the soul has become extinct to itself, extinct to its own extinction, for it becomes unconscious to itself and unconscious of its own unconsciousness ... In relation to the man immersed in this state, the state is called, in the language of metaphor, 'Identity'; in the language of reality, 'Unification'.[60]

This indeed describes the state of no mental content, a complete emptiness, vacuum, void which is typical of the introverted mystical experience. This extinction of the individual leads to unification with the Absolute; as Jalalu d'Din exclaims: 'O, let me not exist! For Non-Existence proclaims in organ tones, "To Him we shall return"'.[61]

By the way of 'negative' mysticism Judaic and Christian mystics have gone beyond the personal godhead to an Absolute which is the unknowable, indescribable, infinite, impersonal origin of all that is. This is in accord with the view of the Absolute that can be garnered

---

[59] M. A. Khan, Sufism in Islam, 2003, New Delhi, p. 201
[60] F .C. Happold, Mysticism, 1963, Harmondsworth, p. 99
[61] E. Underhill, Mysticism, 1911, London, p. 171

from the scriptures and mystical writings of Vedanta and Buddhism, which will be the focus of the next chapter. This leaves Islamic Sufi mystics who point to a state where the self is totally negated leading to an 'extinction of the soul' and a 'unification' with, or 'return to' Him. This state, as shown, is one of no mental content, emptiness, vacuum, void which is typical of the introverted mystical experiences of mystics of all traditions. Ramakrishna showed this by being initiated into Islam and living as a Muslim repeating the name of 'Allah' with great devotion:

> The Master (Sri Ramakrishna) at first had the vision of an effulgent impressive personage with a long beard (Mohammed); afterwards he had the knowledge of the all-pervading Brahman with attributes, and then merged finally in the attributeless Brahman, the Absolute.'[62]

He had a similar experience when practising Christianity although in this case he had a vision of Christ who approached and embraced him, resulting in Ramakrishna losing normal consciousness and merging with Brahman for some time.[63]

These experiences fully convinced Sri Ramakrishna of the validity of both Christianity and Islam, as religions, and also showed him how practising them leads initially to the extrovert 'personal' mystical

---

[62] S. Saradananda, *Sri Ramakrishna the Great Master*, 1978, Myalpore, p. 300
[63] Ibid., p. 339

experiences (through visions) and then to the introvertive impersonal mystical experience of union with the Absolute.

In conclusion, this chapter has attempted to outline the similarities and differences in the way that these Western and Eastern religious traditions conceive the Absolute. They all tend to regard the Absolute as the Source of the Universe, Eternal, Omniscient, Immanent, 'In us', One and Transcendent. These Western traditions regard the Absolute as being personal with human-like qualities but always separate from its creation. Whereas these Eastern traditions regard the Absolute as being impersonal and attributeless but being never separate, in fact constituting, its creation. However, many mystics of these traditions have shown that the One Absolute which is encountered through negative mystical experience appears to be the same. Therefore it could be argued that each of these religions is, as Ramakrishna said: 'only a path leading to (the same) God, as rivers come from different directions and ultimately become one in the ocean'.[64]

---

[64] S .Nikhilananda, *The Gospel of Sri Ramakrishna*, 1942, Chennai, p. 265

Chapter Twenty

The Essential Self

This chapter compares the concepts of 'Self' and 'No Self' in Hinduism and Buddhism, and shows that they each contain streams which posit that awareness is the source, existence and dissolution of all things, that is, the Absolute Reality.

The purpose of this chapter is to compare the seemingly opposite philosophical concepts which lie at the heart of two of the world's major religions, Hinduism and Buddhism, and to show how they each contain 'streams' which arrive at the same realization, outlined by earlier chapters. These concepts are those of *atman*, a Sanskrit word which can loosely be translated as 'The Self' or 'The (essence of a) Person', which is central to Hinduism, and *anatta*, a Pali word which means 'No Self' or 'No essential Person' which underpins Buddhism. The Pali word for *atman* is *atta* and the prefix *an* means 'no' or 'not' thus *anatta* is literally the exact opposite, or negation, of *atman*.

Of course if this were simply the case - that the two concepts were exact opposites, such as 'there is a God' and 'there is no God' - then this chapter would be extremely short, in fact I could stop here! However, the situation is complicated by the fact that there exist many different streams of both Hinduism and Buddhism each with its own interpretation of the concepts of *atman* and *anatta*. As we shall see, some of these are indeed in direct opposition, some in lesser disagreement, and there are cases where the two concepts seem to mean almost exactly the same thing! Not only that, but there are cases where the interpretations of the same concept, within different streams of the one religion, can be seen to be in almost direct opposition. There have been many scholars from both sides who have written on this subject, usually from their own fixed viewpoint. Normally the attempt from the Vedantic (Hindu) side is to show that there is no real difference between *atman* and *anatta* and thus that Buddhism is merely an offshoot of Vedanta. Whereas the Buddhist, especially Theravadan, scholars have been keen to show that the two concepts are complete antonyms of each other and thus Buddhism is a unique religion stemming from the Buddha's rejection of Brahmanism and Vedantic philosophy. Here are examples of these views:

Firstly from *The Message of the Upanishads* by Swami Ranganathananda: 'There is no important form of Hindu thought, heterodox Buddhism included, which is not rooted in the Upanishads.' [65] Then this quote from Malalasekara an active Sinhalese lay Buddhist and statesman: 'This is the one doctrine that separates Buddhism from all other religions, creeds and systems of philosophy ... in its denial of Self, Buddhism stands alone.'[66]

A small clarification is needed here. Brahmanism is the forerunner to the modern-day Hinduism based on the Vedas and the Upanishads. Vedanta literally means 'the end of the Vedas' and is usually taken to apply to those philosophies based on the Upanishads. Stemming from this are the schools of Advaita-Vedanta, Samkhya, Visishtadvaita-Vedanta and Dvaita-Vedanta. So when I am using any of these terms I am considering a form of Hinduism.

In similar fashion Buddhism has spawned many different streams, the main two being Theravada and Mahayana. Within Mahayana Buddhism there are many different 'tributaries' of which I will be considering

---

[65] Sw. Ranganathananda, *The Message of the Upanisads*, 1985, Bombay, p. 18
[66] S. Collins, *Selfless Persons*, 1982, Cambridge, p. 4

Tibetan and Zen Buddhism. When I am using any of these terms I am talking about a form of Buddhism.

To avoid sectarianism and to achieve a certain amount of objectivity, I am going to consider the concept of *atman* (or Self) as interpreted by the four major schools of Hinduism, given above, and then compare that with the concept of *anatta* (No Self) as interpreted by Theravadan, Tibetan and Zen Buddhism.

Before I get started I need to discuss Hinduism and Buddhism in general terms and to clarify a few concepts that will recur during the chapter. Both religions are 'paths of liberation' or ways to escape *samsara*, the continual cycle of death, reincarnation, worldly suffering and death. They both believe in *karma* which is the merit or demerit accrued by your actions. The store, or ledger, of accrued *karma* determines your present and future lives, including the circumstances of your rebirth. Reincarnation occurs because your accrued *karma* will not be exhausted in this life and, generally, all of the actions you perform accrue *karma*, either good or bad. The 'criterion of rightness', which is used to decide whether an action is right or wrong, is whether that action is in accordance with your *dharma*, which is loosely translated as 'duty'. The Hindus and Buddhists have different conceptions of *dharma*, the former believing it to be based on rules applying to class, caste and stage of life (as prescribed in the Vedas and later scriptures), whereas the latter base it on following the Buddha's injunctions and teachings. Both religions believe that one can escape from the 'wheel' of *samsara* by achieving 'liberation' or 'freedom', *moksa* in Hinduism and *nirvana* in Buddhism. The Pali or Buddhist words for these terms are *kamma, damma* and *nibbana,* whilst *samsara* is common to both Pali and Sanskrit.

Finally, prior to the detailed examination of *atman* and *anatta* in the various branches of Hinduism and Buddhism, we need to examine the concept of 'Self', as this will provide a framework within which the comparisons can occur. This is a very complex problem that has been puzzling philosophers and religious scholars throughout the ages but for the purpose of this chapter I am going to break it down into three groups. The first I will call the 'conventional self' to which we all relate when we say 'I'. This is normally thought to consist of the body and mind, the latter consisting of ego, self-image, memories, thoughts, etc. Secondly, we have the 'essence' of the 'individual self' which equates with the idea of 'soul'. This is something deeper than the body-mind (which some philosophers and religions say includes facets of the mind), which is the eternal 'essence' of a person. In systems where this is posited to remain eternally as a unique separate entity I am going to denote this by 'individual self'. Thirdly, in those systems where this is considered to be not separate from the 'Ultimate Reality', Absolute or 'Godhead', and in which liberation occurs by merging this 'essence' back into the Absolute, I am going to denote this by 'absolute self'.

Hindu Philosophical Systems

We are, at last, in a position to consider how the concept of *atman*, the Self, is interpreted by the four major philosophical systems within Hinduism.

Samkhya

Firstly, we will consider Samkhya, proposed by Kapila who lived in ancient times before the composition of many of the Upanishads, which is a dualistic system which posits there are two underlying principles which constitute the universe. These are *Purusa* and *Prakriti*, that is consciousness and nature. Everything in creation comes from, is made of, and finally returns to the one *Prakriti*; compare this with cosmic energy of which, according to the string theory, everything is a manifestation. According to Kapila, behind *Prakriti* is *Purusa*, pure consciousness, the witness, 'enjoyer' or 'enlightener' which is equated with the individual self, or soul.[67] This is infinite and outside of nature but is unique for each person, and thus there are an infinite number of souls or '*atma*'. The argument that supports this is that an individual may gain enlightenment while those around him remain in bondage. Thus Samkhya equates *atman* with 'individual self', not with 'absolute self'. In fact Kapila concluded that there was no Absolute or God, and that *Prakriti* and *Purusa* were quite sufficient by themselves 'to account for everything'.[68]

---

[67] Sw. Vivekananda, *The Complete Works Vol.2*, 1989, Mayavati, p. 455
[68] Ibid. p. 457

Advaita-Vedanta

Secondly, we will consider Advaita-Vedanta 'non-dualism', based on the Upanishads, which proposes that *Purusa* and *Prakriti* are just different aspects of the one Absolute Reality: Brahman. As it says in the *Isha Upanishad*: 'In the heart of all things, of whatever there is in the universe, dwells the Lord. He alone is the reality. ... The Self is one ... To the illumined soul the Self is all. For him who sees everywhere oneness, how can there be delusion or grief?'[69] *Atman,* the term used to denote the essence of each individual, is Brahman, as is everything in creation, and is described in the *Vedanta Wordbook* as: 'The Spirit or Self, the immanent aspect of the Godhead.'[70] This is what lies at the heart of each person or 'conventional self' which is termed the *jiva*: 'The *atman* identified with its coverings body, mind, senses, etc. Ignorant of its divinity it experiences birth and death, pleasure and pain.'[71] One continues on the s*amsaric* cycle as long as one misidentifies oneself with the 'conventional self'. Freedom, *moksa*, is obtained once this misidentification ceases and one realizes the truth that one is the *atman* forever at one with Brahman. It is only the *jiva* that is bound by *karma, dharma* and *samsara*; once *moksa* is obtained the 'conventional self' is seen to be an illusion and thus there is nothing that can be reincarnated. Thus Advaita denies that there is an 'individual self', for in essence we are all at one with the Absolute, and

---

[69] Sw. Prabhavanananda, *The Upanishads*, 1986, Myalpore, p. 3-4
[70] Usha, *Ramakrishna-Vedanta Wordbook*, 1962, Hollywood, p. 16
[71] Ibid., p. 38

thus there exists only the 'absolute self'. This philosophical system was systematised, propounded and championed by Sankara (788-820 CE) who explained that 'the knowledge of the identity of the individual Self and the Universal Self originating from the Vedic sentences such as 'Thou art That' etc. is the means to liberation.'[72]

Visishtadvaita-Vedanta

Thirdly, we come to the system devised by Ramanuja (c. 1056-1137 CE), Visishtadvaita-Vedanta or 'qualified non-dualism'. This teaches that the *atman* (individual Self) is part of the unity of Brahman, but that Brahman has other differentiating qualities. This viewpoint is in contrast to Advaita, which teaches that *atman* is the same as Brahman, and that Brahman is undifferentiated. Thus in Visishtadvaita-Vedanta, whilst the *atman* is part of Brahman it is never the same as Brahman, which has other qualities above and beyond that of the *atman*. In this view Brahman has a personal aspect being 'the repository of an infinite number of blessed qualities' whilst residing *in* everything in the Universe.[73] This is in contrast to Advaita which posits that Brahman *is* the Universe and everything in and beyond it. In Visishtadvaita-Vedanta the self, or *atman*, achieves *moksa* by 'knowing' Brahman but still retains an 'I' consciousness as the 'knower' of Brahman. When this occurs the *atman* escapes from the *samsaric* cycle of birth and death and 'lives with god (Brahman) for ever'.[74] Thus Visishtadvaita-Vedanta

---

[72] Jagadananda, *Vakyavritti of Sri Sankara*, 1973, Myalpore, p. 5
[73] Sw. Vivekananda, *The Complete Works Vol.2*, 1989, Mayavati, p. 247

believes in an essential 'individual self' beyond the 'conventional self', which is the *atman*, but denies that this is the 'absolute self' which is Brahman.

Dvaita-Vedanta

Fourthly, we will consider the Dvaita-Vedanta, or dualist school of Vedantic philosophy proposed by Madhva (1238-1317 CE). Madhva was a realizt who argued that our experience of separation from God and of plurality in general is proof that the *atman* and God are indeed separate. He developed a system which posited five fundamental differences: between Brahman and *atman*, between Brahman and matter, between individual selves (*atma*), between selves and matter, and between individual material substances. Although Madhva claimed that his views came from the Vedas and the Upanishads, he had difficulty proving this and he even went so far as to change the *Chandogya Upanishad*'s famous statement '*tat tvam asi*' (you are That) into '*atat tvam asi*' (you are not That) by carrying over the 'a' from the preceding word! According to this system on achieving *moksa*, liberation, one goes beyond the cycle of *samsara* and after death goes to a heavenly realm where there will be 'eternal happiness and one is in the presence of God for all time and enjoys him forever'.[75] Thus in this system the 'individual self', *atman*, goes beyond the 'conventional self' but is forever distinct and separate from Brahman, the 'absolute self'.

---

[74] Ibid. p. 247
[75] Sw. Vivekananda, *The Complete Works Vol.2*, 1989, Mayavati, p. 243

Summing up the ways that the four major Hindu philosophic systems define the *atman* or 'Self', we find that Samkhya philosophy defines the *atman* as the 'individual self' and denies the existence of an 'absolute self'; Advaita defines the *atman* as the 'absolute self' and denies the existence of an 'individual self'; Visishtadvaita-Vedanta defines the *atman* as the 'individual self' which is united with, but different from Brahman, the 'absolute self'; and Dvaita-Vedanta defines the *atman* as the 'individual self' which is forever distinct from Brahman the 'absolute self'.

All three Vedantic systems believe in a 'conventional self' in which or with which the *atman* resides and it is this which is bound by *karma*, *dharma* and *samsara*. On achieving liberation, *moksa*, the *atman* is no longer identified with this 'conventional self' and transcends the reaches of *karma*, *dharma* and *samsara*.

It is interesting to note that, in terms of categories of essential 'self', Samkhya and Advaita appear to be in direct opposition. However, both believe that behind the manifest world and 'conventional self' there exists omnipresent 'pure awareness' or 'witnessing consciousness'; but Samkhya believes this to be 'many' and Advaita believes this to be 'one'. This difference is crucial, for the aspirant who believes in the 'many', and thus that he/she is unique, can develop what the Buddha considered to be one of the greatest obstacles to liberation, namely 'I-conceit'[76] or 'self-grasping'. Whereas the belief in the 'one', and thus

---

[76] S. Collins, *Selfless Persons*, 1982, Cambridge, p. 94

that we do not exist as a unique separate entities, cannot, if properly understood, cause this.

Buddhist Philosophical Systems

Theravada

It is this belief in a separate, unique, individual essential 'I' that is refuted by the Buddhist doctrine of *anatta* or 'no self'. For it is the clinging to, nourishing, nurturing, protecting and continual considering of this illusory 'I' that causes our psychological suffering and attachment. It is this suffering that is addressed in the Four Noble Truths which are:

> In brief, the five aggregates subject to clinging are suffering.
> The origin of suffering is craving for sensual pleasures, craving for existence.
> The cessation of that suffering is the remainderless fading away and cessation of that same craving.
> The Noble Eightfold Path leads to the cessation of suffering.[77]

The five aggregates, or *kandhas*, constitute the 'conventional self' which is impermanent, ephemeral and continually changing, subject to the cycle of *samsara*. It is fairly apparent that any clinging to something impermanent will cause suffering. In the famous *Anatta-lakkhana*

---

[77] C. W. Gowans, *Philosophy of the Buddha*. 2003, London, p. 31-38

Sutta', which is the 'Discourse on the Not-self' given by the Buddha in Varanasi, he began by stating that the five *kandhas* (form, feeling, perception, mental fabricatts and personal consciousness) are not 'self'. He then went on to ask the monks whether each *kandha*, in turn, is 'constant' or 'not constant'. On receiving the reply 'inconstant' he continued:

> 'Is that which is inconstant is easeful or stressful?'
> 'Stressful, Lord.'
> 'And is it fitting to regard that what is inconstant, stressful, subject to change as: This is mine, This is myself, This is what I am?'
> 'No Lord.'[78]

At this point the Buddha has dismissed the 'conventional self' consisting of the five *kandhas* as being impermanent and 'not self'. However, the question still remains as to whether there exists an 'essential self' within, or behind, the 'conventional self' which is the *atman* posited by the various Hindu schools. Before we consider the Buddha's answer to this question let us finish the discussion on the four noble truths which will show why he answered the way he did. Once one has accepted the truth - that there is no separate, unique, individual 'I' - then there is no 'I' to cling, nor 'me and mine' to cling to. This truth of *anatta* is included in the first point of the eightfold path which is 'right view'. As Alan Watts points out, the 'craving which is to be

---

[78] E. Conze, *Buddhist Scriptures*, 1959, Harmondsworth, p. 188

overcome is more rightly translated as clinging or grasping based on *avidya* (ignorance)'.[79] *Avidya* here being ignorance of the truth of *anatta* and of *anicca*, impermanence. Once there is no 'clinging or grasping' then pain and pleasure are just seen 'as they are' and not clung to or rejected. Thus, although they do cause painful or pleasurable sensations, they do not cause any psychological suffering or frustration as they are not 'mine' and there is no 'me' who they could affect.

What was Buddha's reply when asked by Vacchagotta whether 'the Self' existed? He remained silent. On being asked whether 'the Self' did not exist the Buddha once again remained silent. If he had answered that 'the Self exists' he would have been upholding the doctrine of 'eternalism', and it would have been at odds with his understanding that all phenomena are 'not self'. However, if he had answered that 'the Self does not exist' it would have supported the doctrine of 'annihilationism' which would have been at odds with his own doctrine of *nirvana*, liberation. He also went on to say that all ascetics or Brahmins who contemplate on 'the Self' actually identify this with one of the five aggregates and thus come to the conclusion 'I exist'.[80] Buddha's point is to deny any belief in a personal, unique, individual 'self' which would lead to 'I-conceit' or 'self-grasping' and thus lead inexorably to suffering. However, the question remains: is there anything beyond the illusory 'conventional self' of the five aggregates? Although the Buddha remained silent when asked this directly, we need

---

[79] A. W. Watts, *The way of Zen*, 1957, New York, p. 67
[80] R. Gethin, *The Foundations of Buddhism*, 1998, Oxford, p161

to consider the 'inspired utterance' said to have been made by the Buddha about *nirvana*, which was quoted in the previous chapter.

As Christopher Gowans says, 'This clearly implies that *nirvana* is a reality that stands in sharp contrast to the reality of ordinary experience.'[81] Thus *nirvana* is not annihilation but is beyond all phenomena and manifestation. An interesting question here is that if this is beyond 'personal consciousness', which is one of the five aggregates, then there would be no consciousness of *nirvana*, so how would this be different from annihilation? The answer to this is that personal consciousness, which concerns the mind 'seeing', may not be present, but 'pure awareness', which is the screen on which everything appears (and is 'seen'), is!

The basic Theravadan position, then, is that there is no 'individual self' or 'absolute self', the word 'self' is to be totally negated as belief in any 'self' will lead to 'I-conceit' and 'self-grasping'. On fully realizing this truth of *anatta*, clinging and grasping are completely overcome and one is well on the way to attaining *nirvana*. This 'domain' which one enters on achieving *nirvana* could be likened to an Absolute Reality, although the Theravadans would undoubtedly dispute this.

Mahayana

---

[81] C. W. Gowans, *Philosophy of the Buddha*. 2003, London, p. 149

Next I will consider two later types of Buddhism stemming from Mahayana Buddhism, Tibetan Buddhism and Zen. The terms Mahayana and Hinayana were coined by Mahayana Buddhists to distinguish between the different aims of becoming a bodhisattva or becoming an *arhat*. Mahayana means 'the great vehicle' and was so termed because it is capable of carrying many people to liberation, as a bodhisattva is one who vows not to enter into the final *nirvana* until all creatures are liberated. Hinayana, of which Theravada is considered to be one school, means 'the small vehicle' and was a derogatory term coined by the Mahayanists for those who seek personal liberation, the *arhats*. As Buddhism spread it assimilated, or co-existed, with the religions and cultures it encountered forming many different streams. Tibetan Buddhism has been flavoured by the animism and occultism that pre-existed in Tibet, whereas Zen was formed by the contact of Buddhism with Taoism, and to a lesser extent Confucianism, when Buddhism spread to China.

Firstly I will consider Tibetan Buddhism, which expanded the idea of *anatta* into that of *sunyata* which means emptiness. According to this all things are empty of self or any inherent essence, which means that literally everything is empty, 'like a magical illusion'. Or, to put it another way, everything is just a 'conceptual construct; and has no own-existence, empty of individual primary irreducible existence'.[82] Once again consider the string theory, according to which everything is just composed of strings of energy vibrating at different frequencies,

---

[82] P. Williams, 'Buddhist Thought', 2000, London, p. 134-135

thus nothing has any intrinsic irreducible existence. When everything is realized to be intrinsically 'empty' then all grasping and attachment cease, for there is ultimately nothing to grasp or be attached to, and one is well on the way to attaining *nirvana*. The question now is: does Tibetan Buddhism believe that there is anything beyond the empty world of phenomena, an Absolute or 'Ultimate' reality? It seems that it does in the concept of Rigpa which was explored in the previous chapter and was seen to be 'pure awareness'. From this we can conclude that Tibetan Buddhism denies the existence of an 'individual self', in fact of any 'phenomenal self', and would probably not like the term 'absolute self', but does seem to posit the existence of an Absolute Reality which it calls Rigpa.

Moving on to Zen Buddhism, *Anatta* is listed first among the 'Basic Original Doctrines Essential to Zen' in 'Selling Water by the River – a Manual of Zen training' by Jiyu Kennet. This book comes from the Soto school of Zen and has been blessed by the Chief Abbot of the Sojiji Temple, Yokohama, Japan, which vouches for its authority. Defining *anatta* the author states:

> Apart from mind and matter, which constitute this so-called being that we know as man, there is no immortal soul, or eternal ego, with which we are gifted or which we have obtained in some mysterious way from a mysterious being or force.[83]

---

[83] J. Kennet, 'Selling Water by the River;, 1972, New York, p. 7

The Essential Self

The question once again is, 'does Zen believe in some kind of Absolute (self) which is above and beyond the *kandhas*, the bundle of five aggregates'? It would appear from all the available evidence that the answer is an unequivocal yes. Zen Buddhists talk about 'Zen Mind' or 'Universal Mind' or '(big) Mind' in contrast to the everyday (small) mind which is composed entirely of the *kandhas*. This was also shown, in the previous chapter, to consist of 'awareness' or 'consciousness'. An actual experience of 'Zen Mind' is given by the late modern Zen master Sokei-an Sasaki:

> One day I wiped out all the notions from my mind. I gave up all desire ... and stayed in quietude. I felt a little queer – as if I were being carried into something, or as if I were touching some power unknown to me ... and Ztt! I entered. I lost the boundary of my physical body. I felt as if I was standing in the centre of the cosmos. I spoke but my words had lost their meaning. I saw people coming towards me but all were the same man. All were myself! I had never known this world. I had believed that I was created, but now I must change my opinion; I was never created; I was the cosmos; no individual Mr. Sasaki existed.[84]

This is a classic description of 'absolute self' in which all 'selves' are the same 'Self' and this 'Self' is the cosmos! *Atman* and Brahman are the same 'Self' which *is* everything manifest and unmanifest. It also

---
[84] A. Watts, 'The Way of Zen', 1957, Harmondsworth, p141

supports *anatta,* 'no individual Mr Sasaki existed'. On this evidence we can quite safely conclude that Zen Buddhists do not believe in an 'individual self' but do believe in an 'absolute self', although I am sure that they would not use that phrase.

Summing up and comparison

To sum up, in the Buddhist views and interpretations of *anatta* we find that all three schools deny the existence of an 'individual self'. In Theravadan thought there is no 'absolute self' and questions about an Absolute Reality are not fully answered. I am sure that Theravadans would deny the existence of any such Absolute Reality but in view of the Buddha's comments about the 'domain' which is beyond all manifestation and phenomena, and the supposition that *nirvana* is a real state (or experience?) which can be attained, the question is still left unanswered. When we come to the Mahayanist Tibetan school they would probably deny the existence of an 'absolute self' but certainly hold that there is an Absolute Reality above and beyond the 'empty' world of phenomena, which they call Rigpa. Finally, in Zen thought there exists 'Zen Mind' or 'Universal Mind' which is 'ultimate truth' and is the source of (or beyond) 'small mind', the normal functioning mind. Combine this with the mention of 'the Sacred Self' and 'true self' and I maintain that Zen does accept the existence of an 'absolute self' even if Zen Buddhists would not particularly like this terminology. However, even if we do not use this term then 'Zen Mind' can be equated with an 'Absolute Reality.'

On to the comparison of the various streams of Hindu and Buddhist thought. Samkhya, Visishtadvaita-Vedanta and Dvaita-Vedanta all equate *atman* with an 'individual self' whereas all Buddhist schools interpret *anatta* as denying an 'individual self', so we can safely say that in these cases the concepts of *atman* and *anatta* are in fact in direct opposition. This leaves Advaita which denies the 'individual self'' and equates *atman* with the 'absolute self'. How does this compare with the Absolute hinted at by Theravada and affirmed by Tibetan and Zen Buddhism? Let me make the point that ultimately 'absolute self' and Absolute Reality or 'Absolute Truth' all mean exactly the same thing. In the Upanishads, 'Brahman'and 'Self' are synonymous with the Absolute Reality. However, the Buddha was concerned with the mechanics of overcoming suffering and this was based on the elimination of 'I conceit' or self-grasping, which leads to the end of clinging, grasping and craving. Thus any consideration of a self could only be counter-productive as he asserted that all who contemplate 'the self' actually identify this with the five aggregates. As far as answering questions on the Absolute, he regarded all such questions as unconnected with the goal of overcoming suffering and achieving *nirvana*. In his famous discourse with the sage Malunkyaputta he likened this to a man who, being pierced with an arrow, spending his time questioning the type, make, source and firer of the arrow, rather than just pulling it out.[85]

---

[85] I. B. Homer, 'Cula-Malunkyasutta', 1989, Oxford, p97-101

However, the Buddha's utterance of the 'domain where there is no earth, water, fire, air, wind, sun, moon, etc., which is the end of suffering' is echoed in many of the Upanishads. For example:

> 'Beyond the unmanifested ... is Brahman, the all pervading, the unconditioned, knowing whom one attains to freedom. None can behold him for he is without form. His words cannot reveal, mind cannot reach, eyes cannot see'.[86]

Also, Buddha's contention that those who contemplate 'the self' identify with the 'five aggregates', is directly contradicted by the *Taittirya Upanishad* which says: 'Beyond all sheaths [physical, sensual, mental, intellectual and ego] is the Self.'[87]

It is worth bearing in mind the historical context of the Buddha who lived before many of the Upanishads were written. Williams states that 'the Brhadaranyaka and Chandogya Upanishads were in all likelihood pre-Buddhists; placing them in the seventh to sixth centuries BCE may be reasonable.'[88] Thus it is likely that later Upanishads were influenced by Buddhist thought, as was Sankara some thirteen centuries later. Sankara contrasted *anatta* with *atman* as the difference between the body/mind (which was composed of the five sheaths) and the true Self, Brahman or *atman*. Thus in this definition of body/mind, or the five sheaths, as *anatta* he agrees with Buddha who equates the body/mind

---

[86] Sw. Prabhavananda, 'The Upanishads', 'Katha Upanishad', 1986, Myalpore, p. 37-38
[87] Sw. Prabhavananda, 'The Upanishads', 1986, Myalpore, p. 83-84
[88] P. Williams, 'Buddhist Thought', 2000, London, p. 12

composed of the five aggregates with *anatta*. The major difference is that where Sankara posits *atman,* or 'Brahman', Buddha remains silent.

Moving on to Tibetan Buddhism, we find Rigpa described as primordial, pure, pristine awareness that is at once intelligent, cognizant, radiant, always awake and the nature of everything. In the *Isha Upanishad* we find Brahman, or The Self, defined as bright, formless, omnipresent, self-existent awareness.[89] In this regard, the two concepts of Rigpa and Brahman, or *atman*, are very similar. Brahman is also posited to have manifested itself *as* the universe and thus is the essence of everything, which equates with the Rigpa being the nature of everything.

Similarly with Zen Buddhism, Zen (or Universal) Mind is described as watching (aware), always present, our true nature, the source of all things and ultimate truth.[90] Thus this is also very similar to the concept of Brahman and Rigpa. This is not surprising when one considers that these descriptions are attempts at describing the same indescribable ineffable Truth, or Ultimate Reality, which is revealed on the attainment of *moksa* or *nirvana*. Once again this is validation of that old saying that there are 'many paths to the same goal.'

In conclusion, I have considered the concepts of *atman* and *anatta* as interpreted by various philosophical schools of Hinduism and

---

[89] Sw. Prabhavananda, 'The Upanishads', 'Isha Upanishad', 1986, Myalpore, p. 4
[90] S. Suzuki, 'Zen Mind, Beginners' Mind', 1970, New York, p. 134-137

Buddhism. Those Hindu schools where *atman* is interpreted as an 'individual self' are in complete opposition to the concept of *anatta* which, in all Buddhist schools, denies the existence of an 'individual self'. However, in the case of Advaita, which posits an 'absolute self' which is the same as an Absolute Reality, the situation is less clear. The Theravadan school would probably posit that they were in direct opposition to the idea of an 'absolute self', but they do not totally discount the possibility of an Absolute Reality, leaving the question of its existence or non-existence unanswered. In the case of the two Mahayanist schools considered here, Tibetan and Zen Buddhism, it can be shown that their concepts of Rigpa and 'Zen Mind' have many things in common with the Absolute Reality, Brahman of Advaita. This is not surprising for the 'Ultimate Truth' which is revealed to adepts and mystics of all religions (and their various schools) in their enquiry, contemplation, or meditation must be the same. For by definition there can only be one 'Ultimate' (or Absolute) of anything, or any no-thing!

Chapter Twenty-One

Self Liberation Through Seeing with Naked Awareness

A comparison of our discoveries with the fourth chapter of *The Tibetan Book of the Dead.*

Self-Liberation Through Seeing with Naked Awareness

A friend recently showed me the new complete translation of *The Tibetan Book of the Dead* which has an introduction by the Dalai Lama. The previous translations only contained chapters concerned with dying and what occurs after death, whereas this new version contains chapters concerning achieving liberation whilst alive. You can imagine my delight when I found that chapter 4, 'The Introduction to Awareness: Self Liberation through Naked Perception', deals with awakening through the recognition of pure awareness, which accords almost entirely with what has been discovered in the previous chapters.

This chapter shows how the different paths of self-enquiry, coming out of the Hindu stream of Advaita-Vedanta, and that of Dzogchen Tibetan Buddhism come to the same conclusion without any collusion. The translation used here is by John Myrdhin Reynolds (a Tibetan Buddhist monk called Vajranatha) who has kindly consented to its reproduction from his website www.vajranatha.com. I have deleted some sections which deal with specifically Mahayana Buddhist concepts. In what follows the use of the word 'Mind' represent Universal Mind, pure awareness:

> The Tibetan Book of the Dead, discovered by Karma Lingpa in Southern Tibet in the 14th century, was one of the most important cycle of texts to come out of the Dzogchen tradition of Tibet established in ancient times by Guru Padmasambhava. "Self-Liberation through Seeing with Naked Awareness" is the central meditation text of this famous Tibetan Book of the Dead cycle and is said to have been composed by Padmasambhava

173

himself. It is usually known in the West as The Tibetan Book of the Great Liberation, the title given to it by W.Y. Evans-Wentz (1954). This profound text presents the instructions for the method of Self-Liberation that represent the very essence of Dzogchen, "the Great Perfection," which is traditionally regarded in Tibet as the highest and most esoteric teaching of the Buddha. Directly introducing the practitioner of meditation to the Natural State of the Nature of Mind, which is the contemplative state of pure awareness or Rigpa lying beyond the mind and its mundane operations that constitute *Samsara*, this quintessential teaching of the great master Guru Padmasambhava opens up the possibility to the individual of the realization of freedom and enlightenment within a single life time.

This second edition presents a new translation of the Tibetan text, a commentary on the text by the translator based on the oral teachings of Lama Tharchin and Namkhai Norbu Rinpoche, and an appendix that critically examines the original translation of Evans-Wentz and his erroneous notion of "the One Mind," as well as C.G. Jung's commentary on the latter, where he mistakenly equated it with the collective unconscious psyche.

TRANSLATION OF THE TEXT:

Here is contained "Self-Liberation through Seeing with Naked Awareness," this being a Direct Introduction to the State of Intrinsic Awareness, from "The Profound Teaching of Self-Liberation in the Primordial State of the Peaceful and Wrathful Deities."

Homage to the Trikaya and to the deities who represent the inherent luminous clarity of intrinsic Awareness!

Herein I (Padmasambhava) shall teach "Self-Liberation through Seeing with Naked awareness," from the cycle of "The Profound Teaching of Self-Liberation in the Primordial State of the Peaceful and Wrathful Deities." Truly, this introduction to your own intrinsic Awareness should be contemplated well, O fortunate sons of a noble family!
SAMAYA gya gya gya!
Emaho!

It is a single Nature of Mind that encompasses all of *Samsara* and *Nirvana!* Even though its inherent nature (as *Sunyata*) has existed from the very beginning, you have not recognized it. Even though its clarity and presence has been uninterrupted, you have not yet encountered its face. Even though its arising has nowhere been obstructed, still you have not comprehended it. Therefore, this (direct introduction) is for the purpose of bringing you to self-recognition. Everything that is expounded by the Victorious Ones of the three times in the eighty-four thousand gateways to the *Dharma* is incomprehensible (unless you understand intrinsic Awareness). Indeed, the Victorious Ones do not teach anything other than the understanding of this. Even though there exist unlimited numbers of scriptures, equal in their extent to the sky, yet with respect to the real meaning, there are three statements that will introduce you to your own intrinsic Awareness[91]:

(First, recognize that) past thoughts are traceless, clear, and empty,

(Second, recognize that) future thoughts are unproduced and fresh,

And (third, recognize that) the present moment abides naturally and unconstructed.

When this ordinary, momentary consciousness is examined nakedly (and directly) by oneself,

Upon examination it is a naked awareness,

Free from the presence of an observer.[92]

This direct introduction to the manifest primordial State of the Victorious One is disclosed by the following method for

---

[91] J. M. Reynolds, *Self-Liberation Through Seeing with Naked Awareness*, 2000, Ithaca, N.Y.
[92] Padmassambhava, *The Tibetan Book of the Dead*, translated by Gyurme Dorje, 2006, London, p. 41-42

entering into the practice where there exists no antecedent nor subsequent practices. Kye-ho!

O my fortunate sons, listen! Even though that which is commonly called "mind" is widely esteemed and much discussed, still it is not understood or it is wrongly understood in a one-sided manner only. Since it is not understood correctly, just as it is in itself, there come into existence inconceivable numbers of philosophical ideas and assertions. Furthermore, since ordinary individuals do not understand it, they do not recognize their own nature, and so they continue to wander among the six destinies (of rebirth) within the three worlds and thus experience suffering. Therefore, not understanding your own mind is a very grievous fault. [93]

Be certain that this awareness, which is pristine cognition, is uninterrupted.

Be certain that all that appears is naturally manifested (in the Mind).

There are no phenomena extraneous to those that originate from the Mind.

One's own mind, (when) completely free from conceptual projection, will become luminously clear.[94]

---

[93] J. M. Reynolds, *Self-Liberation Through Seeing with Naked Awareness*, 2000, Ithaca, N.Y.
[94] Padmassambhava, *The Tibetan Book of the Dead*, translated by Gyurme Dorje, 2006, London, p. 44-45

Self-Liberation Through Seeing with Naked Awareness

> In terms of your own mind, as is the case with everyone, *Samsara* and *Nirvana* are inseparable. Nonetheless, because you persist in accepting and enduring attachments and aversions, you will continue to wander in *Samsara*. Therefore, your active *dharma*s and your inactive ones both should be abandoned. However, since self-liberation through seeing nakedly by means of intrinsic awareness is here revealed to you, you should understand that all *dharma*s can be perfected and completed in the great total Self-Liberation. And therefore, whatever (practice you do) can be brought to perfection within the Great Perfection.
>
> SAMAYA gya gya gya![95]

Briefly comparing what we have discovered in the previous chapters with the above (and the quotes in chapter 7), we can see that they both agree that our natural effortless awareness of thoughts and sensations is 'that eternal self-luminous reality' in which forms arise, exist and subside. They both agree that there is nothing to attain, i.e. all striving is unnecessary, all that is required is to recognize the true nature of Mind (pure awareness), and that there is nothing to desire, grasp or get. There is also agreement that this effortless awareness is *here and now*. So all that ultimately exists is this 'pure, radiant, omnipresent field of effortless choiceless awareness' in which everything arises, appears to exist, and subsides without ever any separation or duality.

---

[95] J. M. Reynolds, *Self-Liberation Through Seeing with Naked Awareness*, 2000, Ithaca, N.Y.

Even the title, *Self-Liberation Through Seeing with Naked Awareness*, shows the strong similarity of the two paths, for this is exactly what being 'beyond the separate self' is all about: awakening through identifying ourselves as pure awareness, and then seeing (perceiving) everything with pure (naked) awareness. As soon as we clothe our perceptions with the mind's opinions, judgements, etc., we have nodded off again and thus fallen into bondage.

Appendix

Spiritual Experience

This chapter details and analyses the author's realizations and experiences on a seven-day silent retreat in 1996. This book is based on these realizations and experiences plus those that have occurred during the following twelve years of meditation and contemplation.

Appendix

The spiritual experiences I would like to discuss are my own, which occurred in late 1996 whilst on a seven-day silent retreat. These occurred after thirty years of spiritual search and practice, the last ten of which were as a devotee of the great Hindu saint of the late nineteenth century, Sri Ramakrishna. This entailed two to three hours of daily meditation, *japa* (mantra repetition) during daily activities, reading every word said by or written about him, including daily readings of *The Gospel of Sri Ramakrishna*, and chanting. I then encountered a disciple of Sri Ramana Maharshi, Gangaji, who said 'Stop! Be still, you are already That'. The message being that the effort and search were masking that which is always present; all that was required was to 'stop' and see what is always here. After many years of struggle and effort this news came like a breath of fresh air and I glimpsed the essence, that undeniable ever-present reality. I immediately enrolled on the upcoming retreat and the following experiences (quoted from a letter I was writing to my sister at the time) occurred on the evening of the third day:

> So this is the next day and something pretty amazing occurred yesterday afternoon/evening. I decided to sit and try out this new method whilst waiting for Satsang, to get a spot near the front you need to get there 90 mins. early. I managed to still my mind fairly quickly (I guess my meditation practice helped there) to where the only thought was 'Who am I?' At this point there was no reply. I found myself looking into nothingness where 'I' did not exist! The feeling was that inward feeling

which you get in meditation plus one of peace and joy although these were not put into words as they tend to be in my meditation.

Shortly afterwards Satsang began and I did not have the opportunity to go any deeper. When satsang finished, about 6.30, it was dusk and I decided to go for a walk before dinner. I felt pretty normal as I walked past the buildings, cars and campsites, but then as I turned left and headed out towards the magnificent mountain views/ranges, something amazing happened. I suddenly felt the divine presence all around, the magnificence of the divine *Lila* (or play) of God was almost overwhelming. Then I looked up at the sky and was completely blown away by the gently swirling mass of blacks, greys, blues, gold and white with the full moon, like a gigantic iridescent pearl, giving intermittent *darshan* to all below! I felt completely intoxicated and found myself staggering like a drunkard as I surveyed the amazing scene all around. They say that the *Nitya* (the ground, the centre, or the cosmic consciousness) is indescribable, but I can tell you the *Lila* (or divine manifestation) is also that. Words may try, but they pall into insignificance compared to that divine splendour. The stark beauty of the mountain range and bluffs covered in rainforest, the gently rolling fields and valleys swathed, as it were, in dark green velvet, the trees almost shimmering in consciousness, and above all that sky, the kaleidoscope of divine colour for ever rearranging itself into ever more glorious patterns. I now know what Ramakrishna meant when he said that to get the 'full weight' of Brahman you have to accept both the *Lila* and the *Nitya*. That divine intoxication lasted all evening and a trace of it still remains. I had intended to do some further self-enquiry before I went to bed, but the 'Who am I' seemed pointless and insignificant compared to That.

The next day I was driven out of bed at 3.15 by the chorus of my roommates (ten middle aged men) snoring, and after a shower I went down to the yoga room, where finding a thick mat and a blanket I settled down to some serious yoga. I just lay in divine communion ever aware of the divine within and without. If the previous evening was intoxication, this was bliss, with an ecstatic throbbing of the heart and whole body, which was basked in delight. This lasted for a couple of hours until the 'physical exercise' crew started to arrive. I then returned to that divine walk and I was continually aware of the divine (in the form of 'Mother') all around. Singing in the sublime dawn chorus, blowing gently on my face, displaying her beauty as tree and bush, scudding across the sky tinged silver and gold by the sun, lowing in the fields … everywhere was only 'She'! I felt I knew how St Francis of Assisi felt.

The best way to describe the feeling that accompanies all of this is as being deeply in love with a beloved who is always present, both within and without. It was even accompanied by some of the physical symptoms I experienced the first time I fell deeply in love, a deep throbbing of the heart, queasiness of the stomach and an overall glow and sense of well-being.

At this point if you, the reader, were somewhat sceptical I would not be surprised. Before this retreat I could not have dreamed that such experiences would occur. However, luckily for me, not only do I have the 'knowing' and the change that they produced, which are of course the most important, but also I have the memory plus a written and electronic record, on cassette and videotape, of myself reporting these experiences to Gangaji in front of 300 people.

These are, in essence, two different types of experience, the first acting as a catalyst for the following. The first was an immediate experience of the mystical type. In this all 'otherness' disappeared, in fact 'I' as the ego vanished leaving 'nothingness' or 'emptiness'. Describing this is very difficult for although there was nothing (no things, shapes or forms) there, and thus it could be described as 'empty', it felt 'full' of consciousness, peace and joy.

The experiences that followed were mediated by the beauty of nature and had elements of the mystical and enthusiasm whilst engendering a feeling of ecstasy! I felt charged with divine power but also I felt one with everything. I could only describe everything external as 'Mother' whilst I was the observer and enjoyer of this.

I will now consider the elements of these experiences, continuing with the labelling of them as the *first* and the *following*:

The Believer

Having followed a Hindu path for many years and being fully acquainted with the Upanishads, I was fully convinced that 'I am That'. This belief accorded with the *first* experience. However, I had also been a devotee of Sri Ramakrishna whose spiritual experience was very broad but who, in later years, became an ecstatic devotee of Kali, the divine Mother. The belief here is that everything in manifestation (the *Lila*) is a manifestation of Kali (Mother) whilst the awareness, or witness to, all of this is Siva (the *Nitya*). This accounted for the interpretation of the *following* experiences. In saying this I must point out that Kali and Siva are aspects of the one reality, 'That' (Brahman). Kali being the aspect of creation, preservation and destruction (consciousness in motion), whilst Siva denotes the awareness or witnessing aspect (consciousness at rest).

Characteristics

These experiences did have all of the various characteristics associated with spiritual experiences:

a. Ineffability. As I have already said, the *first* was an experience of 'nothingness' and 'emptiness' but was also full of 'everythingness' and 'fullness'. The *following* were of the whole of manifestation being full of God-presence or 'Mother'. These descriptions may seem flaky and paradoxical, but the point is that no description can do justice to them. To know what I am talking about one has to have had the experiences in question. It's like trying to describe the taste of chocolate to someone who hasn't tasted it, or a beautiful sunset to someone who has always been blind.

b. Knowing. These experiences have produced a profound 'knowing' which has lasted ever since. The *first*, a knowing that I am not the mind/body or ego. In fact in essence I am 'no thing' and yet at one with the totality which includes everything. The *following*, that 'All is That' and that in essence there is no separation between anything in manifestation. This could also be described in the terms of 'all is consciousness'.

c. Transience. The *first* only lasted about ten minutes. However, it is readily glimpsed again, for whenever I ask 'Who am I?' I can find nothing, or no thing. The *following* produced an intoxication which slowly faded over the next year. Moments of this reappear when I am in nature with a still mind, i.e. totally relaxed and at peace.

d. Passivity. In the *first* I felt if 'I', as a separate entity, did not exist and thus had no will of my own. In the *following* I felt as if I was in the presence of a divine power, but also infused with and part of that divine presence. There was no will of my own, just a flowing with and enjoyment of the experience.

e. Timelessness. In the *first,* time totally vanished, did not exist. In this state time is absolutely meaningless. In the *following,* time seemed to have slowed as there was such beauty crammed into each moment. But time, itself, was of no consequence in that there was nothing to do or achieve.

Effects of the experiences

As previously stated, they produced a 'knowing' which has never left. This has left a feeling of being totally 'at home' in the universe, an 'ease of being with nothing to achieve, search for or get.' This has had a profound effect on my life, banishing all existential anxiety and creating the desire to point as many people as possible to the utter simplicity of freedom. To this end I have written an article entitled 'Simply Free to Be' which I am going to publish as a booklet. In fact one my aims in studying religion and philosophy is to broaden my knowledge base so that I can turn the article into a book which will appeal to a wide audience from different religious and philosophical viewpoints (this was written in 2000, nine years before this present book appeared).

Authentification

I reported the first two experiences to Gangaji in Satsang in front of 300 people, the following day. She authenticated them by her delight in the listening and her affirmation that there was nothing left for me to do. They also tally with the experiences reported by many mystics following the 'negative' and 'positive' paths. They are also authenticated (although no such authentification is necessary) by conforming to the elements and characteristics previously described.

Beliefs and Symbols

This brings me to the ways that beliefs and symbols of particular traditions are evident in these experiences. The *first* experience is a classic example from the Vedantic (or Upanishadic) tradition. In this the *atman* (individual) merges into Brahman (the totality). Note also how it is also very reminiscent of the Buddhist idea of *anatta* or no self. In fact both traditions point to the same reality, in different ways, that there is no separate individual self but that we are all part of the 'Totality of Being'.

Appendix

The *following* experiences come out of the tradition of Kali, or Mother, worship. In this the Mother is the creator, preserver, destroyer and the essence of all manifestation. The classic symbol is of her standing on Siva, who is inert, just aware of and witnessing her creation. As previously said, both Siva and Kali are aspects of the totality, Brahman. Thus both traditions have the same basis but emphasise different aspects, one the *Nitya* (internal) and the other the *Lila* (external).

Later Reflections

One further point that I would like to make is that writing this book has been an absolute blessing for me as it has unfolded over the years. The recording of the discoveries, and the honing of the text, has been a joy and has increased and prolonged my periods of 'wakefulness'. On re-reading the manuscript so many times, for editing and verification purposes, I have come to realize that I (the separate self) did not write this at all but that it has come from, and through, this limited manifestation of pure awareness. As such it is bound to contain errors due to the limitedness of the manifestation, but hopefully these will become corrected as further discoveries occur. Thus it will always be 'a work in progress', which is wonderful for it will spur me on to overcome its limitations by further investigation, contemplation and meditation. So I would absolutely encourage you, the reader, to record your own discoveries, and never be totally content with what you have written, so that your record will inspire you and encourage you to deeper investigation/contemplation/meditation.

Glossary

Advaita: non-dual.

Anatta: no self.

Anicca: impermanence.

Arhat: one who seeks personal enlightenment so as to attain *Nirvana* and avoid rebirth.

Atman: Brahman within each individual, that portion of the Absolute in each person.

Avatar: an incarnation of an aspect of the Godhead.

Avidya: spiritual ignorance.

Ayin: the nothingness from which 'everything emerges … and eventually returns there'.

Bhumi: spiritual stage on the Bodhisattva Path.

Bodhicitta: awakening or enlightenment.

Bodhisattva: one who seeks full enlightenment so as to aid others to do the same.

Brahman: the all-pervading transcendental Absolute Reality.

Darshan: the blessing or purification felt in the presence of holiness.

Dhamma (Buddhist): duty, following the Buddha's teachings to achieve nirvana.

Dharma (Hindu): duty, the criterion which is used to decide whether an action is right or wrong.

Dharmakaya: The Absolute Unmanifest Reality that is 'Aware Nothingness'.

Dvaita: dualist school of Vedantic philosophy proposed by Madhva.

Ein sof (or *En-Sof*): the infinite nothingness, the source and final resting place of all things.
Fana: absorption into the Absolute, which al-Junaid of Baghdad interpreted as 'dying to self'.
Hinayana: the 'small vehicle', a derogatory term coined by the Mahayanists for the path of those who seek personal liberation, the Arhats.
Japa: the practice of repeating one of the names of God.
Jiva: the individual self which houses the Atman, and which undergoes rebirth until self-realization (that atman *is* Brahman) occurs.
Kali: the Divine Mother, creator, preserver and destroyer. Sakti, cosmic energy, consciousness in motion.
Kandhas: the five aggregates (form, feeling, perception, mental fabrications and consciousness) which according to the Buddhists make up a human being.
Karma, Kamma: the merit or demerit accrued by your actions and thoughts which determine your present and future lives.
Krishna: an incarnation of Vishnu, the 'preserver'.
Lila: the divine play or manifestation, consciousness in motion.
Mahayana: the 'great vehicle' capable of carrying many people to liberation, as a bodhisattva is one who vows not to enter into the final *nirvana* until all creatures are liberated.
Mara: mind-created demons.
Maya: The power of Brahman, which supports the cosmic illusion of the One appearing as the many.
Moksa: liberation from the wheel of birth and death, self-realization, enlightenment.
Nama: name.

Namah: salutations (to).

Nirvana: Buddhist word for *moksa*, enlightenment, awakening.

Nitya: the Ultimate Reality, the eternal Absolute.

Om: Brahman 'The Impersonal Absolute'; but is also the Logos, The Word, and the 'Ground of Being', in which all manifestation arises, exists and subsides.

Paramitas: perfections to be attained on the Bodhisattva Path.

Prakriti: the manifestation, nature.

Purusa: the witnessing consciousness, or awareness, according to Samkhya unique to each individual.

Rigpa: pure awareness which is 'the nature of everything'.

Sakti: cosmic energy, consciousness in motion.

Samkhya: philosophy proposed by Kapila which posited two fundamental principles, Purusa and Prakriti, as the source of all things.

Samsara: the wheel of birth, life, death and rebirth.

Satchitananda: existence (*sat*), consciousness (*chit*), bliss (*ananda*).

Satsang: association with Truth, normally with a guru or spiritual master.

Sefirot: the stages of divine being and aspects of divine personality.

Siva: universal consciousness when it is at rest, aware of every movement occurring in it, which is 'pure awareness'.

Sunyata: The void, formless awareness, aware nothingness

Tagatha: the Buddha.

The Tao: the ultimate principle; the source, which grows and nurtures all things.

Upanishads: the last works of the Vedas, in which ritual was supplanted by the personal and mystical experiencing of the Absolute (Brahman).

Vedanta: philosophy based on the books at 'the end of the Vedas' i.e. The Upanishads.

Vedas: the most ancient of the Hindu scriptures.

Visishtadvaita-Vedanta: qualified non-dualism., which posits that the *atman* (individual self) is part of the unity of Brahman, but that Brahman has other differentiating qualities above and beyond that of the *atman*.

Bibliography

Chogyam Trungpa, *Cutting Through Spiritual Materialism*, 1987, Shambala, Boston
Collins, S., *Selfless Persons,* 1982, Cambridge University Press, Cambridge
Conze, E., *Buddhist Scriptures*, 1959, Penguin, Harmondsworth.
Cottingham, J., *Meditations on a First Philosophy*, 1996, Cambridge University Press, Cambridge
Cox, M., *Christian Mysticism*, 1986, Aquarian Press, Great Britain
Easwaran, E., *The Upanishads*, 1988, Penguin, New Delhi
Forman, R., *The Problem of Pure Consciousness*, 1990, Oxford University, New York
Gethin, R., *The Foundations of Buddhism*, 1998, Oxford University Press, Oxford
Gowans, C.W., *The Philosophy of the Buddha*, 2003, Routledge, London
Gyatso, G.K., *Ocean of Nectar*, 1995, Tharpa Publications, London
Happold, F.C., *Mysticism*, 1963, Penguin, Harmondsworth
Harvey, P., *An Introduction to Buddhism*, 1990, Cambridge University Press, Cambridge.
Hinnells, J., *Living Religion*s, 1997, Penguin, London,
Homer, I.B., *The Middle Length Sayings Vol 2*, 1989, Oxford University Press, Oxford
Jagadananda, *Vakyavritti of Sri Sankara*, 1973, Ramakrishna Math, Myalpore
Kennet, J., *Selling Water by the River*, 1972, Pantheon Books, New York
Khan, M.A., *Sufism in Islam*, 2003, Anmol, New Delhi
Klemke, E.D., *The Meaning of Life*, 2000, Oxford University Press, Oxford
Maharshi, S.R., *Words of Grace*, 1969, Sri Ramanasramam, Tiruvannamalai
Nikhilananda, S., *The Gospel of Ramakrishna*, 1942, Ramakrishna Math, Chenai
Nisargadatta Maharaj, *I Am That*, 1997, Acorn, Durham NY

Padmasambhava, *The Tibetan Book of the Dead*, trans. by Gyurme Dorje, 2005, Penguin, London

Prahbavananda, Sw., *The Upanishads*, 1986, Ramakrishna Math, Myalpore

Ragnathananda, Sw., *The Message of the Upanishads*, 1985, Ramakrishna Math, Bombay

Reynolds, J., (Vajranatha), *Self Liberation Through Seeing with Naked Awareness*, 2000, Snow Lion Publications, Ithaca NY,

Rajneesh, S., *Bodhidharma*, 1987, Rebel Publishing House, Cologne

Rajneesh, S., *Ta Hui*, 1987, Rebel Publishing House, Cologne

Sarada, S., *Sri Ramakrishna the Great Master*, 1979, Ramakrishna Math, Myalpore

Sogyal Rinpoche, *The Tibetan Book of Living and Dying*, 1992, Harper Collins, San Francisco

Stace, W.T., *Mysticism and Philosophy*, 1961, Macmillan, London

Suzuki, S., *Zen Mind Beginner's Mind*, 1970, Weatherhill, New York

Underhill, E., *Mysticism*, 1911, Methuen, London

Unterman, A., *The Jews*, 1981, Routledge and Kegan, Boston

Usha, *Ramakrishna-Vedanta Wordbook*, 1962, Vedanta Press, Hollywood

Vivekananda, S., *The Complete Works of Sw. Vivekananda Vol 2*, 1989, Advaita Ashram, Mayavati

Watts, A.W., *The Way of Zen*, 1957, Pantheon Books, New York

Williams, P., *Buddhist Thought*, 2000, Routledge, London

Index

A

absolute self, 154
   in Advaita Vedanta, 156–157, 159, 171
   Buddhist views summarized, 167
   in Dvaita-Vedanta, 158
   in Samkhya, 159
   in Theravada Buddhism, 163, 167
   in Tibetan Buddhism, 165, 167
   in Visishtadvaita-Vedanta, 158
   in Zen, 166–167

Absolute, the. *see also* awareness; Brahman
   and absolute self, 156–157
   in Advaita Vedanta, 134–136
   as Brahman, 77, 148, 156, 168, 169, 171
   in Buddhism, 136–140, 168
   in Christianity, 129–131
   as consciousness, 43, 81–82
   created the universe for its enjoyment, 113
   descriptions of, 81, 83, 139, 141
   Eastern and Western comparisons, 140–142
   as *Ein Sof*, 145
   and human equality, 115
   in Islam, 131–134
   in Judaism, 127–129
   and mantra repetition, 79
   and negative way, 79, 142–145
   as *Satchitananda*, 56, 114
   in Sufism, 147
   summary statement regarding, 149

Abu Hamid al-Ghazali, 147
Advaita Vedanta, 134–136, 156–157, 159, 168, 171
al-Junaid of Baghdad, 147
Allah, 131–134
anatta
   as body/mind, 169–170
   Buddhist views summarized, 167
   deepening of, 105
   and emptiness, 164
   and *Nirvana*, 163
   as no self, 104, 151
   and radiant stage, 108
   and right view, 162

    and separate self, 160
    and stainless stage, 107
    and Zen, 165–166
Anatta-lakkhana Sutta, 161
anicca, 104, 105, 162
approaching, stage of, 109
arhat, 164
arrow metaphor, 168
atman. see also body/mind; ego; individual self; self-image; separate self
    and Brahman, 156–158, 166
    Buddha on, 137
    and Madvha, 158
    meanings compared, 168–171
    meanings summarized, 159
    and Samkhya, 155
    as Self, 151
avidya, 162
awareness, 31. *see also* Absolute, the; nothingness; 'what is'
    and body/mind, 19–21, 29, 32–35, 61, 89, 93, 142, 169
    as Brahman, 170
    as choiceless, 20–21
    and detachment, 96
    as effortless, 29
    as here and now, 179
    as home, 61
    as impossible to achieve, 47–49
    investigation of, 20
    mantra repetition and, 78
    and mind, 74, 82
    nature of, 14
    as nothing being of consequence, 67–70
    and nothingness, 69–70
    as omnipresent, 21
    as omniscient, 22
    as ordinary, 59–61
    properties of, 140–142
    as radiant, 22
    relaxing into, 72–74, 86–87, 114–115
    as Rigpa, 170
    as Self, 170
    in *Self Liberation Through Naked Perception*, 173–179
    as substratum, 19–20
    as universal consciousness, 43
    as untainted, 22
    of "what is", 19

awareness, identification with. *see* identification, with awareness
ayin, 144–145. *see also* nothingness

B
Barnes, Hazel, 120
bhumis, 103, 104, 105, 106
Big Mind, 138–139
bliss, 114–115
bodhicitta, 105, 107
bodhisattva, 103–104, 109, 164
bodhisattva path, stages of
   approaching, 109
   Difficult to Overcome, 108–109
   face to face, 109
   gone afar, 109
   joyful, 106–107, 110–111
   luminous, 107–108
   radiant, 108
   stainless, 107
body/mind. *see also atman*; ego; individual self; self-image; separate self
   as *anatta*, 169–170
   as beloved, 115
   and Brahman, 121
   compared to awareness, 19–21, 29, 32–35, 61, 89, 93, 142, 169
   and detachment, 96
   experience of, 19, 38
   identification with, 11, 20, 28, 42, 70, 89, 114, 115, 122
   as self-image, 27, 31
   and self-realization, 114
   and separate self, 98
   trusting, 90, 92
Brahman
   as Absolute, 77, 148, 156, 168, 169, 171
   as *atman*, 156–158, 166
   and body/mind, 121
   defined, 118
   in Dvaita-Vedanta, 158
   in Hindu cosmology, 118, 119, 135
   as substratum, 136
   in Tibetan Buddhism, 170
   two aspects of, 118–119
Brahmanism, as forerunner to Hinduism, 152
Buddha, 107
   on the Absolute, 168
   on *atman*, 121

    and Discourse on the 'Not Self', 161
    on Self, existence of, 162
    and self grasping, 158–159
    silence regarding the Absolute, 136–137, 162–163, 168, 170
    and suffering, 168–169
    Upanishads and, 169
Buddhahood, achievement of, 110
Buddhism, 170
    and the Absolute, 136–140, 168
    and absolute self, 154, 164–167, 170, 171
    and *anatta*, 167
    and Big Mind, 138–139
    Four Noble Truths, 160
    Hinayana, 164
    Mahayana, 103–106, 139, 163–167
    and Nirvana, 137
    philosophical systems compared, 160–171
    Theravada, 139, 160–163, 167, 171
    Tibetan, 164–165, 170
    Zen, 138–139

C

Camus, Albert, 122
Chandogya Upanishad, 158
choicelessness, 20–21
Christian Mysticism, 145–146
Christianity, 129–131
Cloud of *Dhamma*, 106
compassion, 35, 94–95, 109, 113
computer, as mind, 10–11, 85
consciousness, awareness as, 43, 81–82. *see also* awareness
conventional self, 154, 156, 159, 160–161, 162
Cox, Michael, 145–146

D

dark energy, 67
dark matter, 67
Descartes, Rene, 30, 48
detachment, 96
dharma, 153, 159
Difficult to Overcome, stage of, 108–109
Dionysius the Areopagite, 145–146
Discourse on the Not-self, 161
discrimination between real and unreal, 95
Divine Mother, 119

Dudjon Rinpoche, 138
Dvaita-Vedanta, 158–159

E
Eckhart, Meister, 146
effortlessness, awareness as, 29. *see also* awareness
ego, 36, 98, 101, 105, 120. *see also atman*; body/mind; individual self; self-image; separate self
Ein Sof, as the Absolute, 145
emptiness, 164–165
enlightenment, 49–50, 53, 54, 61, 105. *see also* awareness
enquiry, 13, 33, 41–42. *see also* practices
existence, enjoyment of, 114
extinction, as negative way, 147

F
face to face, stage of, 109
form, perception of, 81
formlessness. *see* nothingness
Four Noble Truths, 160

G
giving, 104
God, 95, 118, 125–126
   and Christian mysticism, 146
   in Christianity, 129–131
   in Dvaita-Vedanta, 158
   in Islam, 131–133
   in Judaism, 127–128
   and Kabbalah, 145
   and Sufism, 147
   Western view of, 140
gone afar, stage of, 109
Gospel of Ramakrishna, The, 118
Gowans, Christopher, 163

H
Hinayana Buddhism, 164
Hinduism. *see also* Advaita Vedanta
   and Brahman, 118, 119, 135
   Brahmanism as forerunner to, 152
   philosophical systems compared, 154–160
Holy Trinity, 130–131

I

identification
  with awareness, 23, 49, 51, 86, 89–91, 94–97, 104, 110–112, 114, 116
  with body/mind, 11, 20, 28, 42, 70, 89, 114, 115, 122
  with mind, 36, 61, 91, 107–108
impermanence (*anicca*), 104, 105, 162
individual self, 106–107, 137, 154, 154–159, 159, 163, 165, 167–168, 171. *see also* atman; body/mind; ego; self-image; separate self
Isha Upanishad, 156, 170
Islam, and descriptions of Allah, 131–134

J

Jalalu d'Din, 147
Joad, C.E.M., 30
joyful, stage of, 106–107, 110–111
joyfulness, 104
Judaism, and descriptions of the Absolute (God), 127–129

K

Kabbalah, 144–145
kandhas, 160–161, 166
Kapila, 155
karma, 109, 152, 152–153
Kashyapa, 107
Kennet, Jiyu, 165

L

La-Lavan, David ben Abraham, 144–145
love, 95, 114–115
luminous, stage of, 107–108

M

Madhva, 158
Maha-Sattva, 109
Mahayana Buddhism, 103–106, 139, 163–167
Maimonides, 145
Malalasekara, 152
Malunkyaputta, 168
Mandukya Upanishad, 77–78
mantra repetition, 76–79. *see also* practices
mantra repetitition. *see also* practices
maras, 108–109
Meaning of Life, The, 120

meditation, 105, 108–109. *see also* practices
Message of the Upanishads, The, 152
metaphors
   arrow, questioning firer of, 168
   movie screen, 23
   sculpture, 81
mind. *see also* body/mind
   and awareness, 74, 82, 114
   and Brahman, 136
   ceasing activity of, 56
   as computer, 10–11, 85–86, 92
   Descartes and, 30–31
   as filter, 98, 121
   as flow of sensations/thoughts, 42, 54, 73
   identification with, 36, 61, 91, 107–108
   as instrument of awareness, 33
   and living in the moment, 93–94
   and movie screen metaphor, 23
   obsessive thinking and, 12, 27
   as problem solving device, 15, 85
   and rejecting simplicity, 35
   relation to no-mind, 30
   relaxation and, 86–87
   and seeing things as they are, 12–13
   as still, 121
   still vs rational, 122
   as sufferer, 32, 96, 100
   Universal, 138–140, 166–171, 173–179
mind/body. *see* body/mind
Mind, Universal, 126, 138–140, 166–171, 173–179. *see also* awareness
moksa, 156, 158, 159
morality, 105, 107
movie screen metaphor, 23–24
mysticism, 142–149
   Christian, 145–146
   and Kabbalah, 144–145
   and nothingness, 144–145

N
Nagarjuna, 104
negative way, of knowing the Absolute, 142–145
   extinction as, 147
   as introvertive mystical experiences, 143–144
   and nothingness, 144–145
   and Sufism, 147–148

nirvana, 137, 162, 163, 165, 167, 168
Nisargadatta Maharaj, 41
no self. *see* anatta
nondualism. *see* Advaita Vedanta
nothing being of consequence, 67–70
nothingness, 66, 68. *see also* awareness
   as *ayin*, 144–145
   and negative way of knowing the Absolute, 144–145
   as relative to awareness, 69–70
   revealed by mantra repetition, 76–79
   sensations and, 81
   as stillness, 82–83
now, living in the, 93–94, 122. *see also* 'what is'

O

Om Nama Sivaya, explained, 77–78
omnipresence, awareness as, 21
omniscience, awareness as, 22
Ouspensky, P.D., 30

P

Padmasambhava, 138
pain, acceptance of, 96
paramitas, 104, 105, 106
patience, 105, 107–108
philosophical systems compared, 154–160, 160–171
practices
   accepting 'what is', 92–93
   avoiding identification with thoughts and sensations, 91
   commitment to identification with awareness, 89–91
   living in the present moment, 93–94
   mantra repetition, 76–79
   meditation, 105, 108–109
   relaxing into awareness, 72–74
   as secondary to identification with awareness, 94
   trusting mind/body, 92
Prakriti, 155, 156
Purusa, 155, 156

R

radiant, stage of, 108
Ramakrishna, Sri, 125–126, 148–149
Ramanuja, 157
reality. *see* Absolute, the; awareness; nothingness

relaxing into awareness, 72–74, 86–87, 114–115. *see also* practices
Reynolds, John Myrdhin, 173
right view, 162
Rigpa, 138, 167, 170–171. *see also* Tibetan Buddhism

S
Samkhya, 155
samsara, 152, 154, 158, 161
Sankara, 157
    Buddha, compared to, 169–170
Sasaki, Sokei-an, 166
Satchitananda, 56, 114, 115
Schopenhauer, 122
sculpture metaphor, 81
Self, 156. *see also* absolute self; conventional self; individual self
    and *atman*, 151
    awareness and, 170
    existence of, 162
    Tibetan Buddhism and, 165
    Zen and, 166–167
self-grasping, 158–159
self-image, 11–15, 27, 31, 33–34, 120, 154. *see also atman*; body/mind; ego;
  individual self; separate self
Self Liberation Through Naked Perception, 173–179
self-realization, 114–115. *see also* awareness
Selling Water by the River, 165
sensations
    in awareness, 82
    as contrasted to nothingness, 81
    and relaxation, 86
separate self, 12, 56, 96–101, 113, 160. *see also* body/mind; ego
    and body/mind, 98
    meaning of, 179
silence, Buddha and, 136–137, 162–163, 168, 170
singularity, 118, 119
Sogyal Rinpoche, 138
Stace, W.T., 143–144
stainless, stage of, 107
stillness, 82–83
story, letting go of, 99–100
substratum, awareness as, 19–20. *see also* awareness
suffering, 11, 32–38, 92, 96, 98, 100–101, 137, 160, 168–169
Sufism, 147–148
sunyata, 164
Suzuki, Shunryu, 139

Swami Ranganathananda, 152

T
Taittirya Upanishad, 169
Taoism, 164
Taylor, Richard, 120
Theravada Buddhism, 139, 160–163, 167, 171
Tibetan Book of the Dead, The, 60–61, 138, 173
Tibetan Buddhism, 164–165, 170. *see also* Rigpa
Trungpa, Chogyam, 104
Turiya, 78

U
universal consciousness, 43, 77
Universal Mind, 126, 139–140, 166–171, 173–179
Upanishad, Chandogya, 158
Upanishad, Isha, 156, 170
Upanishad, Mandukya, 77–78
Upanishad, Taittirya, 169
Upanishads
   Buddhism, influenced by, 169
   various, 134–136

V
Vacchagotta, 162
Vajranatha, 173
Vedanta, 44
Vedanta, Advaita, 134–136, 156–157, 159, 168, 171
Vedanta, Visishtadvaita, 157–158
Vedanta Wordbook, 156
via negative. see negative way
vigor, 105, 108
Visishtadvaita-Vedanta, compared to advaita, 157–158

W
'what is'
   accepting, 57, 92–93
   awareness as, 19
   and bliss, 56
   enlightenment and, 55
   failure to see, 16
   and living in regret, 120
   and purity of action, 105–106

as *sat*, 114
Williams, P., 169
wisdom, 105, 109

Z
Zen, 138–139, 164–167, 170, 171

The Author – A short spiritual biography

I was born into a strict, but joyful, Methodist family. From the ages of 11-17 I was sent to a Methodist boarding school, which I left with the conviction that organized Christianity was not for me. I could see that what Christ said about living was wonderful, but that the church did not really promote his teachings rather concentrating on him as our 'saviour' and on the purportedly 'miraculous' facets of his life. It was also very apparent that many so called Christians were not interested in practicing what he taught. This was now 1965 and living in central London during the years of flower-power I experimented with various hallucinogens, finding them very beneficial for opening my subconscious which allowed years of conditioning to pour out. This left me feeling totally 'cleansed' and unburdened, ready to start life anew in a spirit of investigation as to the nature of reality. The psychedelic states also presaged, gave a glimpse of, mystical states which I suspected were attainable through spiritual practices. I then embarked on a study of Gurdjieff and Ouspensky which I found absolutely fascinating and was convinced that self-realization was the purpose of life. However they made the process sound so onerous that (being young, foot-loose and fancy-free) I decided to shelve the whole project temporarily.

It was not until eight years later that I resumed the spiritual search when Janet (my partner) introduced me to my first yoga-teacher, Matthew O'Malveny, who inspired us by quoting passages from the Upanishads, Dhammapada, and other scriptures during the class. He also emphasized the importance of relaxation and meditation. There followed a few years of investigating various spiritual paths including a prolonged dalliance with the Brahma Kumaris (Raja Yoga) whose meditations were wonderful, but whose dogma was very hard to take. We then moved into the country to start a pottery and immersed ourselves in Satyananda Yoga, an organization which had no dogma but taught a wide range of yogic practices. We were both initiated into *karma sannyas* by Swami Satyananda and adopted a yogic lifestyle consisting of asanas, pranayama, yoga nidra, meditation, kirtan and vegetarianism.

During this time I was at a silent retreat when I happened to pick up a volume entitled *The Gospel of Ramakrishna* which introduced me to this amazing being who practiced many spiritual paths, within Hinduism and also Islam and Christianity, discovering that they all lead to the same result. He was then approached by many devotees from these various paths all of whom he was able to teach in their own path, whilst emphasizing the harmony of religions. A few years later I was lucky enough to find an erudite nun in the Sarada Ramakrishna Order, based in Sydney, who initiated me into the worship of this amazing being. This entailed two to three hours of daily meditation, *japa* (mantra repetition) during daily activities, reading every word said by or written about him, including daily readings of *The Gospel of Sri Ramakrishna*, and chanting. I continued this sadhana quite happily for ten years.

I then encountered a disciple of Sri Ramana Maharshi, Gangaji, who said 'Stop! Be still, you are already That'. The message being that the effort and search were masking that which is always present; all that was required was to 'stop' and see what is always here. After many years of struggle and effort this news came like a breath of fresh air and I glimpsed the essence, that undeniable ever-present reality. This was followed by a seven day silent retreat which resulted in my first 'awakening', and also in an ecstasy that slowly faded over the following year.

This book came about from the realization that occurred then and has matured over the following 12 years. During this time I wrote a series of articles, for an e-mail news group, based on my meditations and contemplations, around which this book is based. At the same time I have also completed an honours degree in comparative religion and philosophy, using the insights gained by my spiritual practices to inform my essays. Some of these essays have been adapted to include as chapters in this book.

My honours thesis, together with an essay about Ramakrishna used to highlight the themes explored, has now also been published, and is available from Lulu and www.nonduality.com, entitled:

Humanity, Our Place in the Universe
The Central Beliefs of the World's Religions